Chile's Middle Class

LACC Studies on Latin America and the Caribbean

Published with the Latin American and Caribbean Center,
Florida International University

General Editors
Mark B. Rosenberg, Jorge Salazar-Carrillo, and Richard Tardanico

Editorial Board

Gustavo Pérez Firmat
Duke University
U.S.A.

Evelyne Huber
Northwestern University
U.S.A.

Larissa Lomnitz
Universidad Nacional Autónoma
    de México
Mexico

Roberto Macedo
Universidade de São Paulo
Brazil

Sidney W. Mintz
The Johns Hopkins University
U.S.A.

Alejandro Portes
The Johns Hopkins University
U.S.A.

Alcida R. Ramos
Universidade de Brasília
Brazil

Edelberto Torres-Rivas
FLACSO
Costa Rica

Miguel Urrutia
Inter-American Development
    Bank
U.S.A.

Augusto Varas
FLACSO
Chile

Chile's Middle Class

A Struggle for Survival in the Face of Neoliberalism

Larissa Lomnitz
Ana Melnick

translated by
Jeanne Grant

Lynne Rienner Publishers • Boulder & London

Published in the United States of America in 1991 by
Lynne Rienner Publishers, Inc.
1800 30th Street, Boulder, Colorado 80301

and in the United Kingdom by
Lynne Rienner Publishers, Inc.
3 Henrietta Street, Covent Garden, London WC2E 8LU

© 1991 by Lynne Rienner Publishers, Inc. All rights reserved

Library of Congress Cataloging-in-Publication Data
Lomnitz, Larissa Adler de.
    Chile's middle class: a struggle for survival in the face of
neoliberalism / by Larissa Lomnitz and Ana Melnick.
      P. cm. — (LACC studies on Latin America and the Caribbean)
Includes bibliographical references and index.
ISBN 1-55587-258-1 (cloth)
1. Middle classes—Chile—Case studies. 2. Teachers—Chile—
Social conditions—Case Studies. 3. Teachers—Chile—Economic
conditions—Case studies. I. Melnick, Ana. II. Title.
III. Series.
HT690.C5L66   1991
305.5'5'0983—dc20   91-19118
                                                                                CIP

British Cataloguing in Publication Data
A Cataloguing in Publication record for this book
is available from the British Library.

Printed and bound in the United States of America

The paper used in this publication meets the requirements
of the American National Standard for Permanence of
Paper for Printed Library Materials Z39.48.

*To my brothers, Manuel, Mauricio, and Ilya
for their constant support and appreciation*
—L. L.

*To my friend Ximena Aranda
for her constant encouragement and solidarity*
—A. M.

To all the teachers of Chile
—L. L. and A. M.

Contents

	Acknowledgments	ix
1	Introduction	1
2	The Middle Class	9
3	Social Networks of the Urban Middle Class in the Late 1960s	21
4	A Short Account of Teaching and Teachers in Chile	33
5	The Teachers	49
6	Teachers' Lives: Five Cases	73
	Félix Briones	73
	Sonia Salas	85
	Marcia Vidal	107
	Alvaro Canales	115
	Fernando Morales	137
7	Conclusions	147
	Bibliography	151
	Index	155
	About the Book and the Authors	161

Acknowledgments

We carried out our study of Chile's teachers under a contract with the Programa Regional de Empleo para América Latina y el Caribe–International Labour Organisation (PREALC-ILO). The content and opinions expressed are, however, solely the authors' responsibility.

We would like to express our gratitude to the many friends who made this publication possible. Our thanks are due Victor Tokman, director of PREALC in Chile at the project's inception, for inviting Larissa Lomnitz to contribute to PREALC's research on the Chilean middle class. He was succeeded by Cecilia López, who was kind enough to take the necessary steps to bring the project to life. We are also grateful to Alvaro García and Ricardo Infante for contributing ideas and data in the early stages, and to Victoria Contreras for seeking out the statistical data we needed.

We are indebted to Ivan Núñez, then director of the Programa Interdisciplinario de Investigaciones Educativas (PIIE), for sharing his experience and wide-ranging knowledge of educational problems in Chile and for helping us to find interviewees. Finally, we would like to thank Enrique D'Etigny for reading the manuscript and offering valuable suggestions and intelligent comments.

And of course, we are immensely grateful to the teachers, who were willing to talk about their experiences and feelings, no matter how intimate they were.

Chile's Middle Class

1
Introduction

This is a case study, using anthropological methods, that attempts to illustrate the effects of neoliberal economic policies of structural adjustment on a sector of the middle classes—public sector employees—that until now has been associated with the modernization process in Latin America.

Our hypothesis is that members of this social group have been among the most affected by structural adjustment policies. Not only has their standard of living deteriorated, but also their social status and the symbolic construction underpinning their class identity have been threatened.

Our research aims to cast light on the fate of this sector of the middle class, one of the least known, or rather, one of the least studied, of the groups that have borne the brunt of the social debt incurred by neoliberalism. At the same time, we seek to contribute to a more general understanding of the middle class, and with regard to this, special emphasis is placed on survival strategies based on social networks.

We studied a group of primary and secondary school teachers in Chile. They constitute our empirical reference and, for two reasons, allow us to see clearly the effects of the neoliberal economic policies instituted by Chile's recent military regime. First, as teachers—part of the middle class and employed in the public sector—they exercise one of the most representative functions of the welfare state ("To govern is to educate"). Teachers are the most conscious reproducers of the state ideology, and their role in society is the basis of their symbolic construction as members of the middle class. Second, we believe that the Chilean case is particularly instructive because—after 1973—official ideology centered on the destruction of the welfare state and on implementing a neoliberal policy, after having eliminated possible sources of resistance or negotiation such as labor organizations and political parties.

We are aware of the fact that neoliberal economic policies are not to be found only in Chile. But Chile offers the only example we know where the measures required by the model were implemented so rapidly and in such a way that the population had no possibility of offering any resistance. The Chilean case is particularly interesting with regard to what actually happened to the people. Certainly neoliberal "modernization" imposed a social and human cost that, seen from another perspective, became a social debt; that is, those who paid for it are the state's creditors.

The concept of social debt (*deuda social*) was proposed by PREALC, taking the idea of the late president elect of Brazil, Tancredo Neves, who coined the term when he presented his governmental program during his electoral campaign.[1] It refers to the debt generated within each country with regard to the sectors most affected by economic adjustments to the burden of foreign debt. That the debt is social means that the economic sacrifice demanded from the population to service the foreign debt was not equitably absorbed by all national sectors. In Latin America this social debt is borne not only by the poor sectors (which increased from a third to 39 percent of the population between 1980 and 1985), but also by other groups not considered poor, but whose real income and purchasing power were drastically reduced. These groups include middle-class sectors, both public and private, that were affected by plummeting investment and the subsequent decline in job creation; in short, by economic stagnation (average growth in the region between 1980 and 1985 was 0.4 percent a year).

The investment coefficient during the five years we analyzed went down from 22 to 16 percent in Latin America as a whole. This decreased the creation of formal jobs in relation to the growth in labor supply, which, together with a reduction in services offered by the state (a consequence of the implementation of the neoliberal model), brought about a rise in unemployment; increased employment in sectors with low productivity (in the informal urban sector and the traditional rural sector); an increase of people working in the formal sector of the economy with salaries below the poverty line; a fall in the average income of all salaried classes (between 1980 and 1985 gross income fell by 2.7 percent); lowered social expenditure per capita (this category of public spending was reduced by 9 percent per person).[2] These facts give an idea of the magnitude of the social debt at the regional level. In the case of Chile the adjustment policies implemented to deal with the foreign debt accentuated the effects of the neoliberal economic model that was applied rigorously beginning in 1975.

After 1973 a process of radical change was undertaken in Chile, involving not only the political system but also the economic system and, consequently, its institutions. This was the context into which the neoliberal, or Chicago School, economic theory was introduced. The starting point was a critique of Chile's economic development up to 1973, which argued that there had been stagnation for three main reasons: (1) inefficiency in the assignment of resources caused by protection of national production from foreign competition, and also to excessive state intervention in the economy; (2) an overly large public sector (*estatismo*), meaning the expansion of publicly owned firms and growing state control of private enterprise; and (3) tight regulations that prevented the development of the capital market. To correct this situation, a model based on the following assumptions was implemented: efficient resource assignment must incorporate a free market and the opening up of the economy to foreign competition; public enterprises are less efficient than private ones; economic freedom is the basis of and a prerequisite for political freedom; and the growth of the economy will necessarily benefit all social groups making up a country. Following this model, the military government proceeded to liberalize prices, markets (expressly omitting the labor market), and the financial sector; open up the commercial and financial sectors, allowing foreign participation; reduce the role of the state; and privatize the economy.[3] We will go into detail only regarding the reduction of the role of the state.

In Latin America the so-called *desarrollista* state was the "sociopolitical and economic pivot" of the model of growth and partial modernization implemented during the years following World War II. "[The state] expanded and assumed new and varied functions—job creation, capital accumulation, the creation of public enterprises, the provision of social services (health, education, housing, social security). It also supported private enterprise by means of subsidies, protection, and credit."[4] All this was done on the basis of the industrial development already achieved and the surplus generated by traditional exports. However, these were not enough to sustain growth and fulfil all the functions the state had assumed. Society was coming to demand more and more. "As the surplus ran out, the governments increasingly resorted to inflationary financing and later to taking out loans from foreign sources, the latter process reaching a feverish climax during the 1970s."

The spectacular level of foreign borrowing came to an abrupt end in 1982, when the foreign debt crisis curtailed the state's accumulating and redistributing role. At that point, not only was a source of credit lost, but there was now the need to send large remittances abroad. The policies of economic adjustment were the reply to this situation. They included, on the one hand, reducing imports and attempting to increase exports, with the aim of generating income in foreign currency (this implied reducing income, consumption, investment, employment, and salaries); and on the other, cutting back the public sector as a whole—dismissing public servants, keeping salaries depressed, reducing expenditure on public social services, eliminating subsidies, decreasing public investment, and privatizing public enterprises while attempting to increase the government's revenue.

Since the crisis of the 1930s the Chilean state had been conceived as the body responsible for promoting development, as a fundamental factor in saving and investment, and as the corrector of social inequalities: the welfare state. The growing demands made on this welfare state, and the will to satisfy them, exceeded its resource possibilities, provoking, among other things, the crisis of 1973. Soon after assuming power, the military government began to implement its neoliberal economic policy. Development and redistribution functions were assigned to the market. The concept of the subsidiary state was established, replacing the welfare state. According to this new concept, the state should limit itself to functions such as defining the rules of the game and financing administration and defense, with some social expenditure aimed at compensating for the effects of the market on those living in extreme poverty. This last was called the "focalization of social expenditure." It is hardly necessary to add that these reforms were carried out with the wholehearted support of the military government, meaning that neither criticism nor social cost were taken into account, and that the new measures were simply carried out by force.

The idea that the free market would automatically produce correctives to the early effects of neoliberal restructuring has not been demonstrated in practice. Half the population now lives in poverty, having lost opportunities, employment, and social security.[5] Furthermore, with no democratic interplay, without political parties and labor organizations, the government could impose policies of control and liberalization at the expense of large social groups. The new labor laws and political restrictions left large sectors of the population without any possibility of negotiation. (It should not be forgotten that Chile's competitive position in the international market is determined to a great extent by its low price of labor.) The 1982 foreign debt crisis in Chile fell upon a country laboring under the effects of these policies, and thus the economic adjustment measures generated by the crisis were far more onerous for the Chileans than for other Latin Americans.

The state's new passive role led to a reduction in public investment of more than 50 percent between 1974 and 1982, without any private investment taking its place. Investment was financed by foreign loans, making the foreign debt grow by 29 percent. The negative effects of these new loans were aggravated by the fact that they were not used for productive investment, which might have generated foreign currency to service the debt. They were mainly used to finance the import of consumer goods. At the same time the diminished role of the state led to a decline of 31.5 percent in the number of public employees between 1975 and 1981. The numbers remained stable after 1982.

The effects of the new policies on those at the bottom of society—the putative focus of social expenditure—were dire:

- Per capita public social expenditure fell 13 percent between 1970 and 1986 (i.e., 4 percent more than the decline in the rest of Latin America)
- During the same period public expenditure on education fell from 100 percent to 71.1 percent
- Public expenditure on health declined to 62.2 percent
- Public expenditure on housing fell to 61.4 percent
- Per capita consumption fell 17 percent with respect to 1973
- Average purchasing power went down 15 percent compared with 1970

- In 1980, 15 percent of the work force was unemployed (more than double the historical figure); by 1982 the figure was 30 percent
- In 1982 many Chilean companies declared bankruptcy

Furthermore, production per capita in 1986 was less than in 1970. The rate of productive capital formation was half that registered for any year during the 1970s.

According to United Nations Development Programme (UNDP) data for 1980, Chile had the worst ratio of salaries to industrial profit. The markup index shows the ratio of the final value of production and operational costs, among which are salaries; the higher the percentage index, the greater is the average profit of a country's enterprises. Chile came first among the forty-one countries in the study, with a markup of 60 percent, more than double the overall world average. Another indicator analyzed refers to the percentage of the industrial product accounted for on average by salaries. Chile occupied the penultimate place among the forty-one countries, with 19 percent.[6] In their commentary on these figures, economists García and Uthoff indicated that "in addition to this limited participation of salaries in the industrial product, the services provided by the state that complement the salary received from the company have also been significantly reduced during recent years."[7] In 1986 the loss of purchasing power, compared with the 1978–1981 period, was more than 40 percent, that is, a loss equivalent to a month and a half's salary a year.[8]

Although there are no studies to show how much of this deterioration targeted the middle classes, there are some indicators that suggest that this sector was one of the most affected. In the first place we have the massive dismissal of public employees mentioned above. Then, average education among the unemployed in the area of Gran Santiago has tended to rise, while the percentage of unemployed with low educational levels has declined (see Table 1.1). The figures in Table 1.1 suggest an increase in the level of unemployment among the middle classes, who previously tended to have completed secondary education. Although this is the level with the greatest negative difference (12.9 percent), there were also increases in special education (0.6 percent) and university education (1 percent). From another point of view, while the participation of the poorest groups (40 percent of the total work force) in the gross domestic product (GDP) fell by 6 percent between 1974 and 1987, that of the middle sectors fell by 8 percent. The survey carried out by the Universidad de Chile, used by García and Uthoff, shows that from the 1970s onward average private consumption for the richest 20 percent of the population is almost fifteen times that of the poorest groups, and that 40 percent of the middle-level population has also experienced a 15 percent decrease in consumption.[9]

In 1987 PREALC constructed an index of the single-salary scale of the Chilean public sector (referring to those institutions that use a single scale).

The PREALC index measures the evolution of the gross salaries received by public sector employees, including basic pay and other benefits required by law. The results show that at best salaries paid to public employees between 1974 and 1986 did not rise at all. At worst it is very likely that they deteriorated by as much as 10.9 percent during this period. Among the services that deteriorated were those related to health and education. In general, whichever indexes are used, it is clear that real wages fell dramatically between 1973 and 1986; salaries never again reached 1970 levels, not even in 1981 (the highest point), and in 1986 they were still 15 percent below the 1970 level.[10]

Table 1.1 Educational Level of the Unemployed in Gran Santiago (percentages)

	1970–1973	1974–1976	1977–1980	1981–1982
Illiterate	2.5	3.7	2.6	2.2
Primary school	57.4	58.6	51.0	43.5
Secondary school	29.6	27.8	35.4	42.5
Special education	6.6	6.0	6.5	7.2
University	4.0	3.9	4.4	5.0

Source: Luis Alfredo Riveros, "Distribución del ingreso, empleo y política social en Chile," Working Paper no. 25 (Santiago de Chile: CEP, 1984).

An employment survey carried out in Gran Santiago in 1988 showed that 30 percent of the active population worked in the informal sector.[11] Of this group, 57.8 percent were self-employed, 14.8 percent were the managers of small firms, and 7.7 percent drove motor vehicles. The informal sector employed a large percentage (24.5) of people who had entered secondary school programs and industrial training courses but not finished them; 25.6 percent of those employed in the Programas Especiales de Empleo (PEE) had completed secondary education. Schkolnik and Teitelboim asked whether the interviewees were employed in the occupation they had been trained for; 16.4 percent said they were not. Schkolnik and Teitelboim found the case of preschool and primary teachers particularly surprising; at the time of the survey many were employed as servants, factory workers, and salespersons, while others had opted for setting up small commercial enterprises. All these data seem to indicate that a certain percentage of the so-called informal sector are from the middle classes—people who had lost their jobs in the public and private sectors.

It is worth noting here that, together with the massive sacking of public employees in 1974, the government promoted the privatization of those newly out of work. An initiative called the Plan del Nuevo Empresario (New Businessman Plan) was created that offered to pay six months' salary to whomever voluntarily resigned from his job as of January 1, 1975.[12]

Although it is rather unorthodox, we have included all these data in the Introduction because they provide the backdrop for the lives of the people we studied. Each interviewee's story shows how behind every figure there is an often dramatic concrete situation that cannot be appreciated by looking at a statistical table. We feel that the dramatic quality of many of these situations is intimately related to the fact our subjects belong to a sector of the middle class. Thus, we must now describe the development of this sector and establish its boundaries.

Notes

1. García, Infante, and Tokman, *Deuda Social*.
2. Ibid., p. 26.
3. Flaño, "El neoliberalismo en Chile y sus resultados," pp. 1–5; García, "Reestructuración productiva y mercado," pp. 11–14.
4. The quoted matter and discussion is from Sunkel, "Perspectivas democráticas y crisis de desarrollo," pp. 9–10.
5. See Tironi, 1988.
6. UNDP indicators from *La Epoca* (Santiago de Chile), April 17, 1988.
7. Alvaro García, Andras Uthoff: "Aspectos distributivos de la politica económica en Chile: La necesidad de pagar la devda social." Santiago: PREALC (1988), pp. 8–9.
8. Arellano, "La situación social en Chile," pp. 1–5; Flaño, "Neoliberalismo," pp. 10–50; Rodríguez Rossi, "La distribución del ingreso y el gasto social en Chile"; Riveros, "Distribución del ingreso, empleo y política social en Chile."
9. García and Uthoff, "Aspectos distributivos de la política económica en Chile," pp. 8–9.
10. Ibid., pp. 1–29.
11. Schkolnik and Teitelboim, "Encuesta de empleo en el Gran Santiago," pp. 19–24.
12. Correa Brito, "Evolución de los empleos públicos 1970–1986."

2

The Middle Class

Defining the Middle Class

The definition of *middle class* has always posed great difficulties for social scientists, chiefly because the component groups have varying relationships with the means of production, the basis of the classical definition of social class proposed by Marx. This has meant that even Marxist thinkers have problems arriving at a precise definition of this sector. Its existence is recognized, but the terminology varies.[1]

Weber, while acknowledging some economic aspects of Marxist theory with respect to capitalism, introduced the concept of power as a determining factor in the social structure as well as the means of production. The centrality of power derives from the growing prominence of the state and the bureaucracy as instruments in the implementation of rationality. Weber argued that, in addition to the classes owning the means of production, there are others possessing certain skills (education and knowledge) that are offered on the market as services and become objective factors determining their owners' position in the social structure. Furthermore, there are status groups based on the objective appreciation of a common identity. In other words, Weber thought that class position was not determined just in the labor market, but that there were also groups defined in terms of a consumption pattern and a life-style.[2]

Two groups of sociological theorists have sought to define and analyze class structure in contemporary society. The first holds a Marxian perspective, and is represented by Ralf Dahrendorf, Nico Poulantzas, Antonio Gramsci, and Alain Touraine. They and other twentieth-century Marxists have expanded on Marx's division of society into two classes, while retaining many of Marx's original concepts. The second group follows the sociological model known as stratification theory that originated with W. Lloyd Warner and Paul S. Hunt's 1941 study of a small New England town in *The Social Life of a Modern Community*. Warner and Hunt's work has dominated sociological studies in the United States, most notably those of C. Wright

Mills in the 1950s and, more recently, of Joseph Bensman and Arthur J. Vidich.

In a Marxian context (of conflict), Dahrendorf states that the middle class does not exist.[3] Yet economically speaking there is a new middle class somewhere between the very wealthy and the very poor. Instead of being an entirely new class in its own right, the new middle class is an extension of the division between the proletariat and bourgeoisie. It consists of one-third salaried employees, similar to industrial workers (employees of shops, foremen, highly skilled workers, etc.), and two-thirds bureaucrats who, although earning less than many white-collar workers and even industrial workers, participate in the exercise of authority, leading them to identify with their superiors. Consequently any further division into other classes would not be plausible, if class is defined as Dahrendorf believes that Marx intended. Classes, according to Dahrendorf, are interest groups that emerge from certain structural conditions and operate in a manner that effects structural changes. This leads Dahrendorf to conclude that "the 'new middle class' was born decomposed. It neither has been nor is it likely to be a class in any sense of this term."[4]

Unlike Dahrendorf's complex and heterogeneous description of the middle class, Poulantza's concept of class determination is drawn from economic, political, and ideological components.[5] Poulantzas equates the middle class with the traditional and new bourgeoisie. The traditional petite bourgeoisie includes those engaged in small family businesses and forms of artisanal production in which the direct producer is also the owner of the means of production. The new petite bourgeoisie is composed of "wage-earning employees who do not belong to the working class but are themselves exploited by capital, either because they sell their labor power, or because of the dominant position of capital in the terms of exchange [services]."[6] Poulantzas goes into depth on class division as representative of an extended division between mental and manual labor, referring specifically to Gramsci's "organic intellectuals." The significance of Gramsci's concept was that he extended the idea of intellectuals to include other professionals previously not recognized as having a role in class ideologies.[7] Yet Poulantzas feels that Gramsci's description was not extensive enough to provide a new definition of class.

It is evident that the concept of class includes different elements for different authors. The same difficulty in coming up with a unified concept of class is evident in the work of the social stratification theorists. Initially both schools of thought held to a more economically based determination of class. Warner and Hunt, when they began their study, hypothesized that occupation and wealth would be the primary determinants of class. They concluded, however, that there were a number of other determinants of a person's position in society. Thus, instead of two dominant antagonistic classes in society, they discovered six. This hierarchy that still predominates in many

North American self-perspectives includes upper-upper, lower-upper, upper-middle, lower-middle, upper-lower, and lower-lower classes.

C. Wright Mills drew on the division between an upper- and lower-middle class and explained it in terms of an "old" and a "new" middle class. He argued that the division within the middle class predates the emergence of a new middle class: the old middle class was divided earlier between mercantilism and subsistence farming. This division still exists, yet the number of individuals employed in other professions has grown substantially, to the extent that by the 1940s the old middle class (farmers, businessmen, and free professionals), which constituted 85 percent of the middle class in 1870, represented only 44 percent. The new middle class (managers, salaried professionals, salespeople, and office workers), according to Mills, was growing in size, with the majority of its members belonging to the lower-middle income brackets. Mills believed that the organizational reason for the shift toward and growth of the new middle class is the steady growth of bureaucracy, in which big business is in partnership with big government. The entire structure of society was changing, requiring an increase in the number of individuals who could administer and manage the system, as well as the change in the system. An increase in the number of bureaucrats does not necessarily entail an increase in power, however, for as a manager "you carry authority, but you are not its source."[8] The security that the old middle class found in property, dependent on larger property structures, moved to occupational status; the new middle class now relies on large businesses for job security.

The parallels between Dahrendorf's and Mills's ideas are hard to miss. The distinction that is still maintained is whether or not the sociologist believes that the new middle class should be separated from the upper and lower classes. The idea of the middle class existing as a new class *in itself* is refuted, according to classical Marxist theory.

The contemporary viewpoints of US sociologists further develop the social stratification theory in that they include more individuals in the middle class. In Bensman and Vidich's *The New American Society* there are two echelons of the middle class, the upper and the lower, with one of the primary differences lying in the level of education attained. The upper new middle class is in large part college-educated, "a class of white-collar employees, managers, professionals, junior executives and other service workers in the higher-status services such as education, recreation, leisure, social work, psychiatry and other service occupations."[9]

Some sociologists have sought to synthesize elements of both these models. Touraine, for example, maintains a Marxian perspective, while alluding to some support for stratification theory. He largely rejects the idea of social class, replacing it with political class, adding to Marxian theory the concept of power in the political sphere. According to Touraine, "in the programmed society, directed by the machinery of growth, the dominated class is no longer defined in terms of property, but by its dependence on the mechanisms of engineered change and hence on the instruments of social and cultural integration."[10] While never clearly defining the middle class, he does refer to Dahrendorf and the new middle class. He places additional individuals in Dahrendorf's grouping of bureaucrats in the middle class; that is, the masses of technicians and employees without the power of authority. Touraine appears to accept some elements of the stratification model, rejecting the Marxist position that the new middle class could be an antagonistic element in society. Rather, the new middle class is a product of the "programmed" society, in which the control of information serves as a measure of class. Thus the middle class is confined to working within its organization to protest against injustices within the bureaucracy, as well as to defend its employment status and careers.

In the socialist countries thinkers have emerged who also propose the existence of a new class.[11] These writers apply the Marxist model to the societies of Eastern Europe where the state almost completely controlled the means of production and monopolized the distribution of the social product. They put forward the idea of a dominant class that controls the mass of workers. The Hungarian sociologists Konrad and Szelenyi[12] describe a "rational-technical" system, in which the planning and the distribution of production, the assignment of goods and services, are the responsibility of a group of individuals who legitimize their control of society on the basis of their technical and professional knowledge. These intellectuals (individuals who possess specialized knowledge allowing them to achieve positions of control) are becoming the dominant class in the socialist systems. This proposal is an extension of Marx's model of social class, in which the dividing lines between the two antagonistic classes are no longer defined by the private ownership of the means of production but by political control. Elements of Weber's theory can also be detected in these ideas, especially regarding the role of state power, although it is also true that this is recognized by Marx in his mode of production.

Gouldner takes up the same ideas and generalizes them when he writes about modern society, particularly in developing countries. According to Gouldner, industrialization in the Third World has favored the emergence of a "cultural bourgeoisie" whose capital is the control of education, culture, and technology. The intellectual and technological elites will tend to become a new class that proclaims autonomy from the traditional bourgeoisie and pursues political power.[13] While Gouldner's theoretical approach differs from that of Konrad and Szelenyi, his work parallels theirs both in its arguments and in the general conclusions reached.

When the Industrial Revolution occurred in the Central countries, the nations that were not industrialized found themselves in a dilemma: to join in the process and industrialize; or to interrupt their active participation in history. According to Milovan Djilas, local capital, and the class and parties that represented it, was too weak to solve the problem of rapid industrialization.[14] This was why the revolution and the party that represented it—in the case of Russia at least—became a necessity, and thus it was the state, controlled by a new revolutionary class, that took on the task of rapid industrialization. In this way, the social conditions allowing the reorganization of the country, the initiation of rapid industrialization and capital accumulation, were created. This process led to the state's transformation into the owner of all property (the importance of private property ceased or diminished), and the new revolutionary class, by holding power, came to control property and the social product.

Rudolf Bahro writes that once the capitalist countries industrialized, the others had no other option: if it could not be done through capitalism, it had to be done by means of the state, the so-called "noncapitalist road to industrialization."[15] In the traditional countries the social structure did not allow the emergence of classes or groups that could carry out industrialization; that is, the bourgeoisie did not have the strength to impose the process, as had occurred in the industrialized countries. The only alternative was the appearance of a new class, based on the intelligentsia, that took over the state apparatus and restructured society such that the conditions needed for industrialization were created. The regimes that today are called Communist are nothing more than those who have followed the noncapitalist road to industrialization, by means of the state bureaucracy. On the other hand, in the non-Communist underdeveloped countries the role of the state and its bureaucracy is also observed—but not to the same degree as in the Communist countries—as the body that directs industrialization and social modernization.[16]

Industrialization in Latin American countries developed in unfavorable conditions, the product of rapid socioeconomic change, political instability, and other adverse factors of both internal and external origins. As a result, the state's role changed from being one of regulation in support of the bourgeoisie to one of direct participation in the production process and in the direction of industrialization. Hence an elite promoting economic development and modernization was created, which directed industrialization from positions within the state apparatus.

The new elite came mainly from the middle classes, among whose ranks were the politicians, technocrats, intellectuals, and members of the armed forces who cooperated or competed among themselves for control of the state apparatus. This group was committed to a modern life-style, and their specialist skills became essential for planning and economic development, and for handling the political problems derived from social change. The public employees (civil servants) in the upper echelons of the hierarchy of public administration were usually members of the middle class who had acquired power and assumed responsibility in circumstances that were frequently difficult and precarious.

A long period of technical, professional, or scientific training is a prerequisite for the aspirant to technological leadership. To the extent that technical personnel fulfil these requirements, they have access to political power, and their participation in government becomes greater. As a result, the more advanced a country is in industrial terms, the more the state apparatus expands, and the greater the number of technical and professional roles within that apparatus.[17]

On the other hand, the emergence of industrial consortia and transnational companies implied a demand for professional skills in the private sector.[18] There is thus a direct relationship between the development and evolution of the new middle-class elites and the public universities, since the latter not only transmit the knowledge allowing an individual to legitimize a position in the state apparatus, but also the technological leaders of the future are in the same universities, studying side by side with the political elite.[19] Political leaders and technical cadres are socialized in the same political culture, learning the art of negotiation and establishing the social networks that will form the bases of the principles and alliances of national political culture. Hence the national universities are the seedbeds of the political and technical elites for the state apparatus.

The Latin American Middle Class: A Theoretical Account

Classical studies of the middle class in Latin America encounter the same problem of heterogeneity that plagues those attempting to define the middle class as construct. Researchers agree that the region's middle class has its origins in industrialization and urbanization, and that its development has subsequently been linked with these processes.[20]

J. Johnson proposed the use of the term *middle sectors* instead of middle class, given the heterogeneity of its composition and of its links with the social structure, the variety of segments making it up (employees, urban and rural businessmen, farmers, tradesmen, industrialists, members of the professions, etc.), and the variety of its political behaviors and social objectives. Nevertheless, members of the middle class do share some common interests that group them together. According to Johnson, the middle sectors have come into being and grown along with urbanization and public education. They have contributed to the development of industrialization and the professionalization of the armed forces. Middle-sector growth has been a factor in the expansion of public bureaucracies as their members demanded new jobs, be it through the imposition of more public services or through the intervention of the state in the economy. The social legislation promoted by the middle sectors legitimized a policy of social welfare and facilitated a more equitable distribution of national income. Such policies were accompanied by strong nationalist sentiments that led to an economic nationalism.[21] For Johnson, modernization in Latin America was achieved to a large extent thanks to the middle sectors who laid the foundations of modern societies and economies in the capitalist style. Politically this was achieved through the alliance of these sectors with groups of urban workers. Johnson considers the function of the middle sectors to have been both to modernize and to contribute to political democracy. The middle sectors have been committed to economic development and to innovation and rationality.[22]

J. Graciarena describes different types of middle classes in terms of two typologies. The first distinguishes between dependent and autonomous middle classes according to whether they work for a salary in a relationship of dependency or own and control property and the income from it. The second typology discriminates between the old and the new middle classes. The old middle class is made up of groups formed during the colonial period and the nineteenth century. These groups have very close links with the upper classes—patron-client and dependent relationships. The new middle classes are the product of recent economic development and are found mainly in the modern sector of the economy—industry, commerce, and services. These different types will behave differently in the social and political spheres, and their life-styles and ideologies will differ.[23] The four types Graciarena describes illustrate the heterogeneity we have been talking about. The obvious question is: What is it that makes an ambassador and an employee of the postal service, an immigrant shopkeeper and an executive, a not-too-successful lawyer and a prestigious doctor with a private practice, a schoolteacher who is the son of a peasant and a university professor who is the son of a landowner all consider themselves middle class?

Eugenio Tironi, using some of Bourdieu's ideas on the problem of the social classes, suggests an approach to finding the answer to this question. He starts by recognizing that sociology's obsession with the question of the properties that characterize the middle class as a distinct and distinguishable class leads nowhere, given the fact that a vast and varied conglomerate of individuals describe themselves as belonging to such a class. Rejecting the alternative of denying the existence of the middle class by using precisely the argument of this internal diversity, Tironi proposes looking for a specific mode of constitution and cohesion of the middle class, introducing the notion of a "symbolic identification." He indicates that the mechanisms of aggregation that give form to a class suppose the existence of a core group that exercises a strong attraction over disparate groups, with different properties, who have hitherto been deprived of specific instances of representation. The result of this process would not be a category characterized by homogeneity, but by self-identification of the peripheral groups with the core group, self-defined as middle class. It is a case of symbolic construction built on an act of will. Quoting Boltanski, Tironi points out that—in the case of classes as in that of nations—the more heterogeneous the groups needing cohesion are, the more spiritualist and voluntarist is the unification discourse attempting to represent the group.[24]

The object of reflection in Tironi's work is thus to look at the middle class as a social category, as a nominal identity through which its members classify, typify, and distinguish themselves symbolically from other groups. Since the middle class lacks clearly homogeneous properties (unlike the working class, which shares a position with respect to the means of production), unity is achieved by a process of symbolic unification that constructs the boundaries of the field of reference and the identification of the group. Tironi writes that this is an attempt to explain an identity that obeys neither shared common properties, nor families of similar properties, nor equivalent social trajectories; neither does it respond to an ideological attempt at unification (as in "working class consciousness").[25]

The Chilean Middle Class: A Genealogy

In Chile there is a common notion that the middle class is the product of the state, meaning that public employees are recognized as the core group around which the middle class has organized. This—according to Tironi—confirms Bourdieu's idea of a constructed class; that is, the result of an act of will (state policy) and not of economic relationships that have given origin and identity to the class. The middle class in Chile would thus be the product of an effort to construct the symbolic unification of social aggregates that are materially dissimilar, with political mobilization as its purpose.[26]

Symbolic unification implies establishing the boundaries of the class (that is, distinguishing between "them" and "us"). Belonging to the middle class is *not* belonging to the working class, nor to the upper class, nor to the rich. To the barrier put up by the wealthy themselves, the middle class responds with an idealization of its own status. On the other hand, being middle class is also not belonging to the poor, a sector feared as being sometimes dangerously close. The proximity of the poor explains why teachers are so deeply disturbed by their loss of status: the deterioration of material conditions undermines their ability to go on *feeling* middle class, and the assault on their dignity makes the defense of their symbolic self-construction as members of the middle class increasingly difficult. In the final instance, the symbolic construction is expressed in objective terms: where to live, where and how to be educated, and so on. Given the absence of an objective common identity, based on a material underpinning, the configuration of the middle class comes about through the logic of symbolism. What is interesting about symbolism is that it produces social identity by creating the difference.[27]

Tironi designs a genealogy of the middle class based on the continuous recomposition of capital owned by this sector. According to this idea (also based on Bourdieu), each class is characterized by a given amount of capital, and by the distribution of capital by type in three sorts—economic, social, and cultural. The economic capital of the middle class is personal. It is usually not inherited but is associated with the personal or family labor through which it came into existence. It would thus be correct to speak of a "patrimony" that is economic, social (relationships), and cultural (education, life-style). For this reason, a class must be analyzed according to three criteria: (1) the volume of its overall capital; (2) the structure of the capital, that is, the proportion represented by each of the three sorts; and (3) the core group. The middle class would be defined by the possession of "medium" patrimonial capital, by a diversity of segments, and by high mobility deriving from the use of social and cultural, as well as economic, capital.

Tironi describes the process that gradually led to the grouping of what was to be the initial core group, the peripheral groups that identified with it, and a second core group that finally displaced the first. The origins of the Chilean middle class are found in the emergence of groups of tradesmen, small-scale manufacturers, and employees of the service and public sectors. Its symbolic official origin was Arturo Alessandri's election in 1920. Alessandri consecrated the middle class as an official class. This birth is linked with the evolution of the Radical Party, founded at the end of the last century by groups of liberals in the mining industry. With the passage of time, the party became a proponent of state intervention, drew away from the oligarchy, and sought a new social base (the middle class) that could mediate between the oligarchy and the workers. At the same time middle-sector groups that had come into being as a result of the growth of the public sector, trade, banking, and services began to voice demands for social mobility. The emerging middle classes also found support in the state, not just as a source of employment but also as a provider of an educational system that was open to all and tended to have a homogenizing effect on society. That is to say, the state provided resources to obtain cultural capital, independently of productive processes.

Thus, the original core group that acted as a pole of attraction and recognition of the middle class was formed by the new wage-earning segments that came into being at the end of the last century with the expansion of the public sector, education, trade, and services. A considerable proportion lived in the provinces and shared a positivist-rationalist ideology that was militantly secular (expressed mainly in Freemasonry) and almost anticlerical, distinguishing it clearly from the oligarchy. By means of the public educational system (the high school, or *liceo*, and the Universidad de Chile), the middle classes had access to a cultural patrimony that compensated for their lack of a large economic capital and gave them a basis for aspiring to upward mobility. Finally, this core group was almost completely identified with the Radical Party.

According to Tironi, this new middle class was not only characterized by its lack of economic capital, but also by a similar lack of social capital, an essential among the oligarchy where questions such as "who do you know" and "to whom are you related" were particularly important. For this reason, the group devoted itself to cultivating its cultural capital, making use of the public educational system. Cultural capital was later converted into social capital through technical and political positions of privilege within the state. Eventually, cultural and social capital permitted an accumulation of economic capital.

Peripheral subordinate groups, the Catholic group and the immigrant group, with no identity of their own, congregated around the core group of public servants. The Catholic group was composed of young university students who had received a private education, were from Santiago, had broken with the oligarchical values of the Conservative Party, and had been influenced by the new, progressive Catholic ideas. They put aside their original social capital and valued the acquisition of a cultural capital instead. They differed from the core group in their origins and their religious beliefs, and transmuted their cultural capital into economic patrimonial capital. The immigrant group was composed of recent immigrants to Chile (from Europe and the Middle East) who worked in the private sector (trade). With no initial capital, they began by accumulating a small economic patrimony that they invested in cultural capital for their children, translating finally into social capital, converging with the Catholic group. Eventually, the original secular core group was displaced by the Catholic group as the hegemonic group of the middle class dominating the state apparatus.[28]

During the military regime it appears that there were attempts by the state itself, derived from the application of the neoliberal model, to shift the hegemony in the middle class toward individuals practicing free enterprise. This voluntarist construction is supported by the official propagation of an ideology postulating privatization, free enterprise, and individualism as the factors without which modernity and development are impossible.

We would like to put special emphasis on the idea of social capital, following Lomnitz's research on the use of social networks in complex societies.[29] In a study on the Chilean middle class carried out in 1968, Lomnitz found a system of reciprocal exchange of bureaucratic favors that, on the one hand, marked a level of equality and belonging to the same class, and on the other, operated as a system of solidarity for the conservation of status. In other words, social relations represented an important economic resource. In later studies of different social classes (the informal sector and upper classes in Mexico) Lomnitz established that, while reciprocal-exchange social networks were present within each group, the structure of the networks themselves (size and composition) and the types of favors (goods and services) exchanged varied according to the needs of each group or class. In the following chapter, we will summarize the research done in Chile in 1968, so that it can serve as a basis for comparing the structure and use of networks we found in the case of teachers. We will see that the changes in the living conditions of this group are reflected in the use and constitution of its social networks.

Notes

1. Giddens, *The Class Structure of the Advanced Societies;* Gramsci, *Prison Notebooks;* Poulantzas, *Las classes sociales en el capitalismo actual;* Touraine, "Las clases sociales," pp. 3–72; Wright, *Class, Crisis and the State.*
2. Weber, *Economía y sociedad,* pp. 41–44; see also Giddens, *Class Structure,* pp. 33ff.
3. Dahrendorf, *Classes and Class Conflict in Industrial Society.*
4. Dahrendorf, *Classes and Class Conflict in Industrial Society,* p. 56.
5. Poulantzas, *Las classes sociales en el capitalismo actual.*
6. Ibid., p. 251.
7. See also Konrad and Szelenyi, *The Intellectual on the Road to Class Power.*
8. Mills, *White Collar,* p. 80.
9. Bensman and Vidich, *The New American Society,* pp. 5–6.
10. Touraine, *The Post-Industrial Society,* p. 54.
11. Amalrick, *Will the Soviet Union Survive Until 1984?*
12. Konrad and Szelenyi, *The Intellectual on the Road to Class Power.*
13. Gouldner, *The Future of Intellectuals and the Rise of the New Class.*
14. Djilas, *The New Class.*
15. Bahro, *The Alternative in Eastern Europe.*
16. Bottomore, *Elites and Society.*
17. O'Donnell, *Modernización y Autoritarismo.*
18. Stevens, "Mexico's PRI," pp. 227–250.
19. Lomnitz, "Carreras de vida en la UNAM," pp. 18–22.
20. Graciarena, *Poder y classes sociales en el desarrollo de América Latina;* Hoselitz, "El desarrollo económico de América Latina," pp. 49–65; Johnson, *Political Change in Latin America;* Ratinoff, "Los nuevos grupos urbanos."
21. Johnson, *Political Change in Latin America,* pp. 28–29, 209–218.
22. Ibid, pp. 223–224.
23. Graciarena, *Poder y classes sociales en el desarrollo de América Latina;* see also Hoselitz, "El desarrollo económico de América Latina."
24. An example of this can be found in the work of Claudio Lomnitz on the role of ideology in the construction of modern Mexico.
25. This was confirmed by a December 1989 survey carried out at a national level by the Center for the Study of Contemporary Reality of the University Academy of Christian Humanism. Interviewees were asked which social class they belonged to; 42.7 percent said they belonged to the middle-middle class, 33.3 percent said they were lower-middle class, and 22 percent said they were lower class. Only 2.9 percent said they belonged to the upper-middle or upper class.
26. Tironi, "La clase construída."
27. Bourdieu, *Le sens pratique,* quoted in ibid., p. 6.
28. Ibid., pp. 9–17.
29. Lomnitz, *Como sobreviven los marginados;* Lomnitz, "Reciprocity of Favors in the Chilean Middle Class"; Lomnitz and Pérez Lizaur, *A Mexican Elite Family, 1820–1980;* and Lomnitz, "Informal Exchange Networks in Formal Systems."

3

Social Networks of the Urban Middle Class in the Late 1960s

The typical member of the middle class we studied in 1968[1] was either a public servant, a private employee, or a liberal professional. His or her access to the state apparatus depended to a large extent on a network of political, social, and family connections. These networks operated a system of reciprocity that consisted of the continuous exchange of favors; an ideology of friendship motivated the exchange. The favors tended to be bureaucratic and usually consisted of preferential treatment in dealing with red tape or priority access to one of the services offered by the state, setting aside the rights and priorities of third parties. While informal exchange of a reciprocal nature is also found in other social classes, the structure of the networks and the favors exchanged in these cases respond to other needs and resources.[2]

According to an informant, networks were a form of help used "to obtain something more easily and in less time." He added that "the objectives are usually legal, although the way they are achieved can be irregular. These favors are given and received in a spirit of friendship and without feelings of guilt. However, the person conceding the favor is always conscious of the future benefit it may bring him, a friend, or a relative of his."

The following example (mentioned by another informant) may clarify the essential features of the system. "A judge, whom we will call A, had a daughter who was looking for a job. A friend, a lawyer we will call B, helped the girl get a job with his brother, C. Several years later C wanted a marriage annulled. Legal divorce does not exist in Chile; annulments are legally valid but require proof of some technical error made in the original contract. Therefore, the success of the legal procedure depends to a great extent on the goodwill of the judge. Judge A—reciprocating the favor he had received years before—arranged that the case come before a judge favorable to divorce. Of course, no money changed hands during the entire episode."

This system, which at the time was disparagingly called *compadrazgo*, consisted of a tacit dyadic contract, or a chain of such contracts between persons linked by mutual friends who act as intermediaries. It is important to note that the initial favor is granted without any specific idea of how it will be returned. It is rather that the required reciprocity is held in reserve for future use, should the need arise.

Types of Favors

The services that were obtained through these social networks included, among others, employment, bureaucratic favors, education, and access to the influential.[3]

The most frequent way of getting a job, particularly in the public sector, was by using contacts. Looking for a job entailed a mental review of all personal relationships until one hit upon a friend with some link to the personnel department of the specific agency where employment was sought. In the same way, when some position opened up, a list of relatives and friends would be gone over until the appropriate candidate was found. The following comment, attributed to President Carlos Ibáñez, illustrates the process: "Between a relative and a friend, I prefer the relative; between a friend and a stranger, I prefer the friend." This system could be considered the principal mechanism for assigning jobs, since even people with the highest qualifications preferred to be backed by a contact and did not just count on their objective merit when applying for a job.

Obtaining bureaucratic favors was the most common use of compadrazgo. Such favors included expediting certificates, permits, passports, and numerous other types of documents, normally entailing a considerable waste of time and bothersome red-tape procedures. These favors had varying importance and included obtaining import licences, customs facilities, exemptions from military service, and loans.

In the same way, the network was used to get places for children in prestigious public or private schools. Middle-class parents were very aware of the value of a good school for their children, since their school friends would become important and lasting social connections. The school was a source of friendship that extended the area of social interaction outside the family, and that might go beyond barriers of class, sex, and national origin. A friend who helped to get a child into the desired school thus elicited considerable gratitude and provided a highly valued favor.

Similarly, social introductions to influential people and potentially useful contacts were also thought of as very special favors.

Compadrazgo played an important role in Chilean politics as well. Various informants said that even the Chilean political party system was largely based on this type of relationship. There are well-known politicians who came into the public eye thanks to their group of personal followers.

However, there were favors that could not be had through this system. According to one informant, "any favor which goes against the ideology of friendship and decency [is excluded]. To try to have sexual relations with a woman after doing her a favor is considered totally unacceptable behavior. Any activity that goes against the standards of the middle class, such as robbery, murder, taking advantage of women or defenseless persons, and, in general, any act that violates dignity and contravenes honorable behavior" are taboo. Such acts would destroy the idea of friendship, degrading it by making it into complicity. The system thus possessed its own moral code that limited the possible favors and also the returns. Although these values are not held exclusively by the middle class, the above quotation reveals that they are part of its moral code, forming part of its symbolic self-construction.

Rules of Reciprocity

The commitment to reciprocity acquired on receiving a favor tended to be stronger than any written or legal document. And any lack of reciprocity was morally sanctioned: "to fail to return a favor is as dishonest as taking an object and not paying for it; a case in which someone receives a favor and then does not return it when it is needed, and when he is able to do so, is never forgotten. However, this rarely occurs."

In spite of its importance, reciprocity was not mentioned openly. Also, a person who was never in a position to reciprocate stopped asking favors if he wanted to maintain a relationship of equality. Similarly, a person with experience in the use of this system would try to measure his requests so as to avoid both taking on too many obligations and owing favors to undesirable people. However, an established relationship would not last if the persons involved did not exchange favors from time to time. If the relationship were to be maintained, it had to be periodically activated, even if only with small favors. Asking for such favors gave the friend to understand that he too could ask for a favor when he wished.

Another rule of reciprocity was that gifts and payments of any sort were excluded. To offer either of these would have been taken as a personal offense, since the exchange of favors was between equals. In the same way, when a favor was requested in return, there were rules of conduct that avoided mutual discomfort. For example, the desired favor was suggested or insinuated in the form of a request for advice. This gave the person to whom the request was addressed the opportunity to offer the favor, if he were in a position to do so.

The use of the system required a lot of tact and a discerning eye. The friend whose resources and possibilities were inferior to one's own should not have been asked for anything beyond his/her capacity. Yet s/he should have been given the chance to reciprocate; otherwise his/her pride would have prevented him/her from asking for future favors. On the other hand, a powerful contact should not have been bothered with trivial requests: the services sought should have been in accordance with rank.

The degree of familiarity or social distance between the persons exchanging favors could lead to variations in the rules of reciprocity described above. It was not the same to approach a relative or an intimate friend as it was to approach someone who had been reached through other contacts (see Figure 2.1). In all cases feelings of friendship and of common liking (*simpatía*) were essential; in any case the category of friend or relative comprehended many degrees of social distance.

Figure 2.1

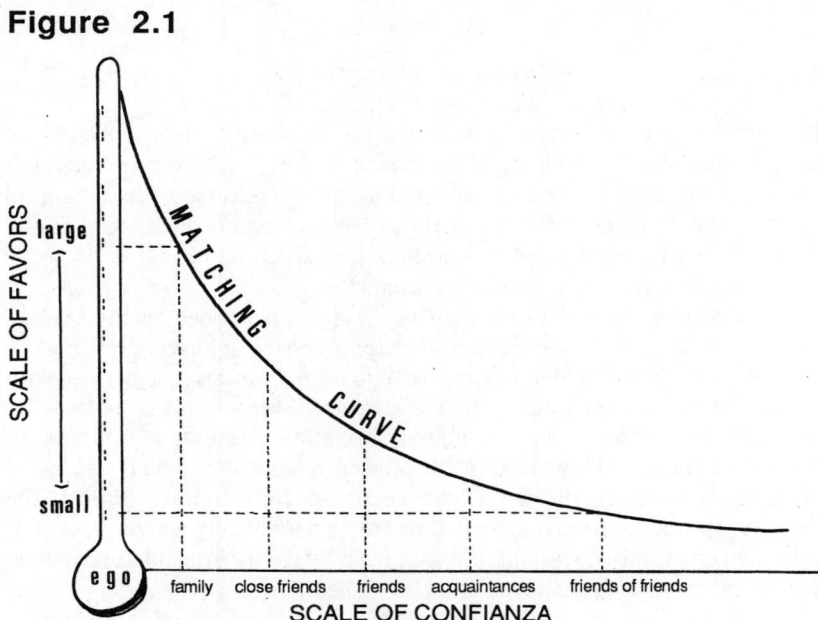

Members of the Network

Essentially, compadrazgo was a personal relationship between individuals who considered each other of the same social level. As a result, according to one of our informants, contacts were sought among "relatives, members of the same political party, friends, acquaintances of the same social level, friends of friends, work companions, members of a Masonic lodge, or, in general, people sharing the same intellectual aspirations, the same political ideology, or similar interests in life." This list comprehends people who think of themselves as equal in terms of the middle-class ideology of friendship.

Why was the use of this system limited to the Chilean middle class? Each class has different resources and needs. The middle class was in the position of offering and receiving favors of a bureaucratic type. A member of the working class could not reciprocate this type of favor, and a member of the upper class would not be prepared to undertake such an exchange, since to recognize equality with a member of the middle class would imply a loss of status. As a result, when two individuals from different social classes were concerned, the exchange would take on a different form, because the elements of reciprocity within the context of sociability characterizing the system were lacking.

But, given the heterogeneous composition of the middle class, and thus the hierarchy within it, a gradual transition between the middle classes and the adjacent social classes could occur, giving rise to ambiguous situations like the following example, provided by a high-level public official. "Once I happened to require a service from a modest office girl in a government office. The favor consisted of obtaining an immediate copy of a certain document that would have taken a couple of weeks through the normal channels. Of course, a direct offer of money was out of the question, yet I would have been only too happy to have paid for the favor and I had the idea of taking her a small gift. Imagine my surprise when the young lady refused to accept the present and suggested instead that I take her out to supper. She was an unsophisticated girl but naturally I couldn't refuse. The next evening she appeared with a friend; the three of us went to a good restaurant and my companions ordered a large meal, probably the best meal they had ever eaten."

This example suggests the following conclusions: the official offered an immediate material reward because he felt that the social distance between himself and the office girl was too great, vertically, for them to be able to have a social relationship; by rejecting the payment in money, the girl put herself at the same class level as the official; she did, however, accept a material payment, but one that was delayed by one day and that consisted of a personal invitation. In this way, the reciprocity conformed, at least outwardly, with the middle-class ideology of friendship.

Various reciprocal-exchange situations can be described by simplified models. The ideal model, that is, equality of access to the services run by the state, operates in effect in exchange for the payment that the employee receives for his work; as a result, the model does not include the exchange of favors, since theoretically they are unnecessary. A system of informal exchanges that coexist with formal trade-offs can also be modeled: this combination of friendship and services occurs only between equals. With other social classes, the nature of the exchange is altered, since the element of friendship and the symmetry of resources does not enter into the situation. With the lower classes, the favor is returned with loyalty and gratitude. With the upper classes, it is reciprocated through graft, that is, the market, as it is paid for.

The institution of compadrazgo can be interpreted as an expression of solidarity aimed at the survival of a social group. A member of the middle class should seek the largest possible number of friends located strategically in the different levels of both the public and private administrations. It was, therefore, absolutely necessary to extend the network of relatives, incorporating friends, relatives of friends, and friends of friends. Thus, each member of the middle class was at the center of an extensive network of personal relationships interconnected by ties of both family and friendship.

Values and Attitudes

Most of our informants revealed a certain ambivalence about the use of their networks. They tended to be reticent when talking about the personal benefits they had obtained, especially when these were of a financial, political, or legal nature. They spoke far more freely of bureaucratic favors. However, the majority agreed that compadrazgo should not exist in an ideal society. Important differences appeared in the degree of rejection. Some explained compadrazgo as a response to scarcity, and pointed out that it develops positive traits of friendship and mutual assistance. But on the other hand, the unfairness for third parties and even for society in general was recognized.

This ambivalent attitude appears to have been based on the underlying conflict between the ideology of class solidarity and of responsibility for one's own kind on the one hand and the liberal ideology of free enterprise historically adhered to by the middle class on the other. Although the universality of rules and the ideology of free enterprise based on individual merit were recognized, in practice the government official found himself sought out by relatives and friends and felt he could not let them down. For this reason, friendship and group solidarity often took precedence over individual merit. And though the losers felt that their theoretical rights had been threatened, and they were granted the right to protest, an excessive show of resentment was seen as useless, ridiculous, and in bad taste. The ideal attitude of a loser was described by one of our informants: "when I fail to get a job because someone else has better connections than I have, I don't let myself be bitter; I realize that in time I too will have friends in a position to help me in life." In fact, competition was seen as a necessary evil, a result of the shortage of resources, but it was not valued as a means of testing the worth of an individual. The struggle for existence was competitive, but it tended to be fought for in groups and not individually. Thus, the fact of losing did not affect the individual's self-image, as might be the case if success depended exclusively on personal merit.

On the other hand, the ideology of friendship was egalitarian: "anyone can have friends." In Chile, this ideology was cultivated from childhood and reinforced throughout life. Children were encouraged to visit and to play with the children of their neighbors, their school friends, the children of relatives and friends of their parents. During adolescence they shared secrets with intimate friends, and once they became adults they tended to share each of life's incidents in the company of their friends. Chilean middle-class families normally had an intense, hospitable, and informal social life; friends called around without any prior arrangements. To have a lot of friends was not only a source of pleasure but also of prestige and popularity. Chileans who lived abroad (probably like any transplanted group) missed these shared experiences and those of pitting their personal resources against the system within the stimulating context of group solidarity. Chilean friends were said to have outstanding "human" qualities, including the willingness to help a friend in need.

The degree of ambivalence about compadrazgo could also depend on certain differences within the middle class. (The grouping of dissimilar social categories attracted by a central core group described previously should be remembered here.) In general, rejection seemed to be more explicit among the upper-middle class (children of the upper class and of middle-class European immigrants). However, although one member of this group called it a "shameful institution," he confessed that he had made use of it to "jump" the bureaucracy, since not to have done so would have been like "committing suicide."

* * *

From the point of view of economic anthropology, the different types of transaction and exchange of resources, labor, goods, and services in a society are analyzed in terms of three basic forms—reciprocity, redistribution, and market exchange. Each of these is contained in specific institutions inserted within the overall set of social relationships.[4] Chilean compadrazgo was an institution of reciprocity, not so much in the form of a balanced exchange of one favor for another, but rather as a relationship of variable social distance that was associated with the exchange of variable favors. Furthermore, this exchange of favors indicated an individual's belonging to the Chilean middle class.

According to the model proposed by Marshal Sahlins, there is a continuum between one extreme—generalized reciprocity (that is, voluntary and permanent aid across time, without any open stipulation of reciprocity or of specific periods of time within which favors should be reciprocated)—and an opposite extreme—negative reciprocity (wherein the question is simply how one person can take advantage of another). In the middle of the continuum is balanced reciprocity. From the moral point of view, the continuum goes from the most positive, which is altruism, to the most negative, which is egoism. "The intervals between them are not only degrees of material equilibrium in the exchange, but also *intervals of sociability*. The distance between the poles of reciprocity is, among other things, the social distance."[5]

The relations of Chilean compadrazgo constituted, in the first place, a spectrum of institutionalized reciprocities in a modern, urban society. Figure 2.2 represents the continuum of social distance from the point of view of a middle-class person (Ego). The reciprocal exchange of favors induced by friendship occurs only on the horizontal axis, representing membership of the middle class. The names that typify social distance within the middle class (close friends, friends, acquaintances, etc.) are categories Ego uses to classify his relationships. An individual can pass from one category to another: an acquaintance can become a friend; a friend can become a close friend and even a relative. On the other hand, the inverse can also occur: a friendship can cool or break down completely.

Let us now look at the types of favors that were exchanged within the institution of compadrazgo. The variety was so great that it is difficult to

Figure 2.2

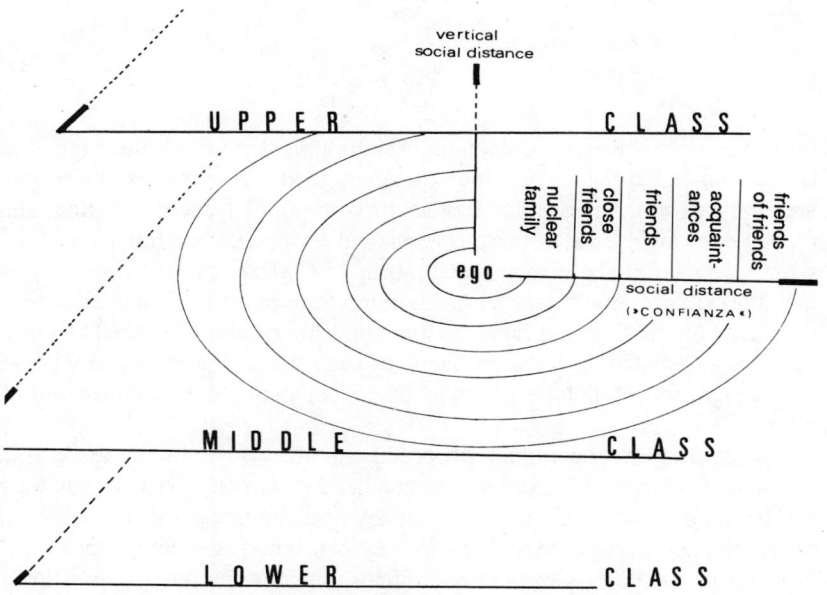

classify them. However, there was a mental scale of favors that Ego used to approach the need to solve a given problem. The use of this system to solve problems implies the operation of matching up the diagram of social distance with the type of favor required (see Figure 2.1). In this way Ego's strategy ("Who is the most appropriate friend to ask?") was clearly influenced by social distance.

Furthermore, there was no purely static correlation between the type of reciprocity and social distance: each influenced the other. While social distance determined the type of favor sought, the request itself and its corresponding result could change the two friends' position on the social scale: an acquaintance could become a close friend by granting a particularly valuable favor; and a friend could become a simple acquaintance by not fulfilling the expectations corresponding to his initial position on the social distance scale.

As well as the horizontal differentiations of social distance (intraclass), we should also look at the vertical or interclass social distance. True reciprocity of friendship and favors is practiced only between social equals. If there is an exchange of favors between individuals from different social classes, the mode of exchange is qualitatively different and reflects differences in power and position.[6] We found two new institutionalized forms of exchange, according to whether the member of the middle class did a favor to a member of the working class or to a member of the upper class. The first is *redistribution,* and was associated with a type of political boss (patron-client relationship). The second is *market exchange;* for example, bribery. In the first case favors were exchanged for political votes; in the second they were exchanged for money.

In conclusion, the system of exchange of favors and friendship was both generalized within the middle class and sensitive to differences in social position. The requirements included social equality and a type and level of employment compatible with the exchange of favors. We thus propose that participation in this reciprocal exchange constituted an indicator of belonging to the Chilean middle class.

Redistribution and Market Exchange

The political influence of the middle class appeared in 1968 to be related to certain characteristic forms of exchange. Many of our informants said that the Chilean system of political parties in general, and the Radical Party in particular, was based largely on compadrazgo. To give a rough outline of the mechanism: a political figure used his position in the bureaucracy to do numerous favors for his friends. Eventually the number of these clients and the range of such reciprocal relationships increased until they included people who could reciprocate only with gratitude and political adhesion. Such a situation of unbalanced exchange led to the acquisition of power as a result of the possibility of benefiting politically from the favors granted. The favors were converted into votes. This process was gradual, and formed the basis of the political clientelistic relationships characterizing the various political parties with access to the public administration of the state. In turn, the politician acquired or accumulated power that could then be converted into resources to be distributed among his supporters. In the language of Polanyi, this system is called redistribution.

It is significant to note that this type of politician arose in the parties of the middle class. Redistribution began to occur as horizontal social distance went beyond the candidates' circle of friends and acquaintances and eventually included members of the lower classes as well. There are well-known examples of political bosses who managed to consolidate an independent group of supporters in this way. These were not the only type of politician to emerge in Chile, and they became less common as Chilean politics became more dominated by parties with a well-defined ideology. However, the history of Chile's middle-class governments could be analyzed from the point of view of a redistribution of social and economic benefits to the middle and lower classes.

Market exchange, on the other hand, represents the opposite extreme. An individual could also sell favors for money to members of the upper class when social distance was very great. In such cases any personal relationship or friendship was considered impossible. Acceptance of a bribe recognized class inferiority, since it excluded the possibility of having friends in common or of offering some sort of reciprocity. On the other hand, selling services represented the secularization of an institution that, albeit informally, had an almost sacred content of sociability: the family and friendship. This is known as corruption and is opposed to the institution we have described as compadrazgo.

Bribery is essentially a form of market exchange: a mutual material benefit obtained by means of "a free and informal contract."[7] But here too there were stages of transition from compadrazgo to bribery corresponding to more of the many differences in social distance.

The New Situation

Institutional change in Chile also meant that middle-class political parties lost their control of public administration. These parties were the representatives of the type of state that sustained the growth of the middle class. Public administration became controlled by another sector of the same class (the armed forces), which was involved in other social networks, traditionally separate from the political and civilian networks. It is reasonable to assume that the Radical Party middle-class compadrazgo, or the Christian

Democrat variant that followed it, continues to exist with the same basic characteristics: systems of reciprocal exchange between friends and relatives; and administrative-bureaucratic favors, with their own rules of etiquette and their own ideology of support.

The modernization undertaken by the military government after 1973, and more specifically a little later on after the implementation of neoliberal economic policy, has affected the middle class in different ways. Although the middle sectors are mentioned when talking about the social debt, the comments tend to be rather en passant, without any attempt to measure in depth just how much the middle class has been affected by this policy or its ideological accompaniment. The study we have carried out on one sector of the middle class, schoolteachers, shows that at least the members of this social group suffered violent upheaval as a result of their passage from the public to the private sector, the deterioration of their income and working conditions, and the shrinking of the social resources that allowed them to remain in the middle class. This also affected their symbolic self-evaluation with respect to their position in society; that is, what in the final reckoning had allowed them in the past to put up with the economic difficulties that have always beset this sector.

The case of the schoolteachers, as we will see, sheds light on this part of the middle class and shows what their life has been, and is, after the orthodox implementation of the socioeconomic model of adjustment; in a word, how members of the middle class are also creditors of the country's social debt.

Notes

1. Lomnitz, "Reciprocity of Favors in the Chilean Middle Class."
2. For the poor social groups, see Lomnitz, *Como sobreviven los marginados;* for the upper class, see Lomnitz and Pérez-Lizaur, *A Mexican Elite Family, 1820–1980.*
3. We are writing in the past tense since we have no data on what happens at present in the public sector. It is reasonable to suppose that the system continues to operate in a similar fashion, although the groups with access to this resource have changed.
4. Polanyi, Arensberg, and Pearson, *Trade and Market in the Early Empires.*
5. Sahlins, "On the Sociology of Primitive Exchange."
6. Blau, *Exchange and Power in Social Life.*
7. Bohanan, *Social Anthropology.*

4
A Short Account of Teaching and Teachers in Chile

As the school is, so shall the entire nation be. — Gabriela Mistral

In May 1989 the principal leader of the Colegio de Profesores (Teachers' Association), summarizing one of the main objectives of the group of candidates he would lead in the forthcoming elections of the association, said that they would seek to "maintain [their] fight to reconquer the dignity of Chilean teachers, through the promulgation of a genuine Estatuto Docente [teaching statute] that would guarantee fair pay, job stability and fluid access to courses for perfecting professional skills." He added that they wanted to make education once again the object of preferential attention from the state and that "there might be a joint effort [on the part of the Colegio de Profesores and the future democratic government] to provide all Chileans with a modern and efficient educational service, founded on respect for the dignity of educators and on the participation of the educational community."[1]

This brief summary of teachers' aspirations reveals what they perceive as the profession's net losses during the years in which the neoliberal model ruled supreme, after 1973—fair pay, job stability, access to further training, and participation in the formulation of educational policy.

In 1971 teachers represented 14.8 percent of the workers in the tertiary sector and 20 percent of all public employees, thus constituting one of the largest labor groups in the country. As a profession, teaching had a qualitative importance based on the following factors:

- Teaching was rooted in a national educational system in constant expansion; and teachers provided one of the services most solicited by the population.
- The sector's professional training was a product of an old and proven system of teacher training. (For example, the Instituto Pedagógico was founded in 1889 as part of the Universidad de Chile; by 1892 the first twenty-nine students had graduated.)

- Teachers were early organized into a professional association, one of the largest and most active within the Chilean labor movement.
- Teachers carried political weight, not only because of their electoral significance but also because of their social activity, influence on local communities, and capacity to produce members of the political elites (governors; members of parliament; local, regional, and national party leaders, etc.).[2]

From their beginnings as a professional group in the early years of this century, teachers expressed their opinions on educational policymaking, not just by commenting on the government's proposals, but also by putting forward their own. To an important, and perhaps determining, degree, this contributed to the expansion of the educational system, the relative improvement in teachers' salaries, the democratization of educational opportunities, and many of the reforms and innovations in the field of education.

In accordance with the function they fulfilled in the educational structure, there were different types of teachers, going from the preschool level to scientific-humanistic high school education, passing through basic elementary school and technical-professional training courses. There was an ad hoc course for each one of these; however, "together with the graduate teachers, there was always a variable proportion of teachers who had spent some time in the teacher-training schools without finally graduating. There were also others with incomplete training, or who had studied other subjects at university level or who were simply high school graduates."[3]

Private education had a similar structure, but the vast majority of Chilean teachers worked in the public sector (in 1973 the figure was 80 percent). Even in 1979, 75 percent of all teachers were still in public education. In the private sector, apart from teachers with a similar training to those in the public sector, 25 percent belonged to a religious order. The schools charging no fees constituted 70 percent of the private establishments; the remainder were divided between those subsidized by the state and fee-charging schools.

As public employees, teachers in the public sector came under the Estatuto Administrativo that governed public administration. This statute gave all public employees, including teachers, a series of rights, among which we would like to point out job stability; health care; rights to severance pay (*deshaucio*), a retirement pension, and a pension fund for widows and orphans; and the right to the free exercise of citizenship and to express opinions on political matters.

Teaching posts were filled by presenting for examination the different candidates' educational background and previous experience to commissions of high-level public employees. The commissions then proposed three candidates, one of whom was finally appointed by the Ministerio de Educación. This was the general norm, although there were some exceptions.

Teachers could not move up the occupational ladder within teaching itself; they had to opt for either directive positions or administrative work. But regarding their pay, they did have the possibility of earning more, since they had the right to a bonus according to seniority, which meant a 40 percent increase on the basic salary after three years of service, followed by successive triennial raises. Possession of a degree also meant a 25 percent bonus.

The number of working hours was also defined: thirty hours of teaching a week were expected of primary teachers, and thirty-six of high school staff. In the latter case, there was also the system of what in Chile are called *cátedras*, under which the total thirty-six hours are divided into sets of six— four sets to be spent in the classroom and two to be used for other educational activities and curricular planning.

A similar statute regulated teaching in private schools, except regarding job stability. While pay in this sector was subject to agreement by both parties, there was a fixed floor as well as adjustments according to seniority, both regulated by law.

Professional associations of teachers were born at the beginning of this century in the form of mutual societies and educational study groups. The two concerns of Chilean teachers can thus be observed as present from the outset: on the one hand the interest in improving their own living conditions; and on the other the desire to improve education itself. When more-militant unionism developed during the 1920s, the teachers' organization achieved "positive advances in the social, professional, and cultural conditions of teachers, while at the same time [it] gave impulse to an integral educational reform."[4]

It is possible that this recognition and validation, on the part of teachers themselves, of the social function of education is one of the reasons why teachers have always had a lower income than other public employees or professional people with the same level of education. Public funding for education was not only allocated to pay the teachers but also to expand and improve the system. And this was understood by teachers as a group. The efforts of the association barely managed to compensate for the loss of purchasing power caused by inflation. "This situation was structurally conditioned: the increasing demand for education meant that a growing fraction of the surplus administered by the state had to be assigned to the expansion of the system's capacity; that is, to the building of schools, training and hiring more teachers, purchasing educational equipment, et cetera, rather than to the improvement of wage levels. It was not possible to assign much more to salaries within the limits of economic development, without altering the balance and consensus that were features of the state's role as 'arbitrator' at the time."[5]

Traditionally, then, the teacher has visualized the state as the driving force behind the country's progress and the agent responsible for development, and himself—as part of the state—as coresponsible for progress and development. As we will see later on when we analyze the interviews with teachers, this way of looking at the functions of the state and of the teacher persists. Our informants object to the privatization of education because of what it has meant for them in terms of their loss of rights and the subsequent deterioration of their living conditions, but they also express their concern for the quality and the future of education in Chile.

The Changes

A first consequence of the advent of the government of the armed forces was the military's intervention in the educational system. With the purpose of "cleaning up" the system and eradicating politics, especially Marxism, from the teaching profession, thousands of teachers were dismissed.[6] Many others were detained by the new authorities, some were executed, and others passed into the category "missing after detention." Along with the direct sacking of staff, there was also the Decreto-Ley No. 6, promulgated by the military junta on September 12, 1973, which read "from this day onward, the personnel of the services, agencies, organizations, companies, and other institutions under state administration, be they centralized or decentralized, will be considered as having temporary appointments."[7] New appointments or nominations automatically meant the termination of the temporary ones, defined as such by the decree-law, and the automatic dismissal of those holding them.

During the early years after the military coup, until 1978, the position of minister of education and some other top-level posts in the ministry were held by members of the armed forces. The educational network in the city of Santiago was divided into various sectors, each one controlled by a military unit. The overall control of the whole of the school system of Gran Santiago remained in the hands of the Comando de Institutos Militares. The strong control exercised by the military, affecting the entire country—which varied from the forcible occupation of school premises to the summons of teachers, ordering them to present themselves at military establishments—had a terrorizing effect and prevented the manifestation of dissenting opinions or opposition on the part of the teaching profession.

The silencing of teachers as a group was also facilitated by dismantling their union, the Sindicato Único de Trabajadores de la Educación (SUTE), and of other professional organizations whose legal status was cancelled, in addition to the closing of Congress, the dissolution of political parties, and, in general, the restrictions on rights of association and expression.

However, the military regime did not escape tradition, and it too had its discourse exalting the function of the teacher. While it destroyed the teachers' organizations and prevented their participation in educational policymaking at any level, the regime questioned the term *educational worker* and proposed to recognize the professional nature of the educator. The new government founded the Colegio de Profesores in 1974–1975 and later, in 1978, designed a Carrera Docente (Teaching Career), a sort of professional service structure. The leaders of the Colegio de Profesores were appointed by the authorities until 1986, when teachers regained the right to elect their leaders. Later another organization came into existence, the Asociación Gremial de Educadores de Chile (AGECH), which strongly opposed the official position. It managed to create a space for itself and even obtained legal recognition. AGECH was voluntarily dissolved when the association became democratic.

The so-called Carrera Docente did not satisfy teachers' aspirations. Not only did it increase the number of working hours and suppress permanent tenure, leaving teachers subject to the possibility of being transferred anywhere, but it did not mean better salaries or matching teachers' status to that of other professions in the public sector. Finally, teachers' qualifications were left to be judged exclusively by the schools' directors. In general, the Carrera Docente was established without participation of teachers themselves either in discussion of the project or its implementation.[8]

The desire to exalt and ennoble the function of education, however, appeared repeatedly in official discourse. In 1974 General Augusto Pinochet proclaimed that "each teacher, because of his vocation, is a true modeler, a guide, a master. The present government fully recognizes the transcendental importance of his mission." Such sentiments did not translate into improvements in pay, or increase educational expenditure on the part of the government. The figures show that the Ministerio de Educación was dramatically affected by the contraction of public spending, which, in the educational sector, was reduced by 24 percent. Education was among the five ministries that lost most personnel. By 1986 it had only 74.2 percent of the number of staff it had employed in 1973.[9]

On Table 3.1, one sees the deterioration in pay between 1972 and 1981, both at the elementary and at the high school levels. The loss was greater for the teacher of long standing than for the new recruit.

The progress and refinement of the neoliberal model implemented in the economy as a whole finally reached the educational system, which, together with social security, health, labor, et cetera, also had to be "modernized." In March 1979 the Directiva Presidencial sobre Educación Nacional was made known and sent to the Ministerio de Educación, accompanied by a letter. Both directive and letter pointed out the new emphases, criteria, and priorities in education (their correspondence with the economic model will become clear below). The basic ideas aimed at the virtual privatization of education; that is, the principle that the state should be a subsidiary agency in society was to be applied in the educational sector—public commitment was to be reduced and private initiative was to take on a greater role.[10]

Table 3.1 Teachers' Pay
(in April 1981 Pesos)[a]

Type of Teacher	Years of Service	January 1, 1972	April 30, 1981	Percentage of Decline
Elementary[b]	0	13,002	11,036	84.8
	30	31,204	21,883	70.3
High school[c]	0	17,527	13,670	77.9
	30	42,066	26,268	62.4

Source: Programa Interdisciplinario de Investigaciones en Educación (PIIE), *Las transformaciones educacionales bajo el régimen militar* (Santiago de Chile: Publicaciones PIIE, 1984), p. 160.

Notes: a. The calculation was made using the official INE index, which underestimates the decline. In 1972 total pay was subject to taxation. In 1981, in the case of elementary school teachers with zero–thirty years of service, only 9,983 and 17,192 pesos, respectively, were taxable; in the case of high school teachers, the corresponding figures were 11,378 and 20,056 pesos.

b. In 1972 each teacher was expected to work thirty "pedagogical" hours (of forty-five minutes each); in 1981 the requirement was thirty chronological hours.

c. In 1972 teachers were expected to work thirty-six pedagogical hours; in 1981 the corresponding figure was thirty chronological hours.

The central ideas of the directive, because they directly affected teachers' working conditions, are summarized below.

• To education is assigned the objective of training "good workers, good citizens, and good patriots," proscribing what the document calls the "politicization" of teaching. The military government reserves all rights of tuition with respect to the content of education.

• The social responsibility of the government in the educational sector is restricted to elementary education. The objectives of such education are that pupils learn to read and write; learn to add, subtract, multiply, and divide; get to know about the history and geography of Chile; and learn their rights and duties in the community. High school and college education are considered a privilege for the youth that achieve these levels, and thus this "exceptional situation" should be paid for.

- The possibility of expanding the educational system is transferred to the private sector. The government preserves "its normative and supervisory functions at all times," but at the same time expresses its intention of putting an end to any expansion of the public sector in the area of education.
- Technical-professional education at a middle level is to be more closely linked to the private sector, subordinating this type of education to the logic of private enterprise as the only criterion of influence in the economic development of the country.
- General criteria regarding higher education and the need to revitalize the collaboration of the Centros de Padres y Apoderados (Centers of Parents and Guardians) with the school system are proposed, emphasizing the necessity of guaranteeing the exclusion of politics. Some initiatives to stimulate teachers' work are proposed.

Some of the measures announced in the directive—with respect to grants for further training and the creation of a Premio Nacional de Educación (National Education Prize), for example—were carried out. Some modifications were also introduced into the Carrera Docente, which in the long term amounted to nothing, since when all the publicly run schools were handed over to the *municipalidades* or to the *corporaciones privadas*, the Carrera Docente became effectively obsolete. The application of Decreto-Ley No. 2.345, on "the debureaucratization of public administration" to the teaching profession had a similar effect on the Carrera Docente. This decree-law enabled the minister of the interior to order the dismissal of any public employee on the grounds of the need to rationalize state administration.

Once they passed into the municipal system or into a subsidized private school, teachers came under the Código del Trabajo (Labor Code). This meant that each teacher was hired as a "worker," putting an end to any attempt to define teaching as a profession and thus giving the activity more "dignity."

The diversification of the norms relative to the training of teachers in the various universities or professional institutes had further effects in the same direction. This diversification occurred despite the dispositions of Decreto-Ley No. 353 (March 15, 1974), which established norms for a national system of teacher training. "In practice, each university continued to design its respective pedagogy courses without any concern for a unified curriculum. Thus, with time, the length of the courses, the content of the curricula, the proportion and organization of the components of the professional training in pedagogy, and specialization, became increasingly varied."[11]

An important concomitant factor was that pedagogy was excluded from the list of university-level degree courses established by a DFL No. 1 of 1981. This meant that teacher training was no longer reserved for universities but could be provided by other kinds of higher-educational organizations, such as professional institutes or academies. Since these new academies were not expected to fulfil "the highest level of excellence"—reserved for the universities by this DFL No. 1—teachers perceived this situation as degrading to the profession, as a lack of recognition of the importance of their function: they felt their professional dignity was being belittled and their status lowered.

The Instituto Pedagógico de la Facultad de Filosofía y Educación of the Universidad de Chile, Macul campus, was separated from the university and first converted into the Academia Superior de Ciencias Pedagógicas. Later, in 1985, it became the Universidad Metropolitana de Ciencias de la Educación. When the future of the institution is considered, many people support the idea of returning the ex-institute to the Universidad de Chile: "whatever the internal organization adopted, this great academic center, which was the Pedagogical Institute, should at least be placed under the aegis of the University of Chile. The quality of teaching and the dignity of future professionals require that it should be so."[12]

Privatization

Up until 1973 there were about three hundred private schools subsidized by the state that were regulated by an ad hoc legislation supervised by the Cámara de Diputados. In 1980 the subsidy was fixed per pupil and expressed in *unidades tributarias mensuales* (UTM; monthly tributary units). This meant that the more pupils there were, the greater the subsidy. According to the educational authorities, this regime of subsidies is "a strong incentive to retain pupils, since it pressures the administrators to guarantee the attendance of the pupils."[13]

However, the measure has also provoked a distortion in the system, since for the educational establishment the retention of pupils became a goal to be achieved at any price, if the school was to survive and make money. This is reflected in the "flexibility" of the evaluations of the pupils' work, leading to an almost automatic pass to the next level. The distortion is also seen in the existence of false attendance lists that have given rise to several scandals.

At any rate, after 1980 the system expanded in an inorganic manner. There are now about two thousand subsidized private schools, many of which are grouped in chains belonging to a single owner.[14] In research carried out by the Colegio de Profesores on 115 establishments, published in 1988, it was found that eighty-three schools (75.4 percent) had contracts with their personnel that were out of date or did not contain the minimum stipulations. Teachers' pay in this sector varies widely. Toward the end of 1988 salaries were between 16,000 and 35,000 pesos for thirty chronological hours.[15]

Municipalization

Two trends came together to shape the course of municipalization. On the one hand there was the general process of decentralizing various sectors of the state apparatus, and on the other there was the desire to act in accordance with the principle of a subsidiary state. The state was to take charge of only those activities the private sector could not or would not take on. Municipalization was seen as a first step, since the municipalities went on to create the corporations that actually took charge of education. There was only one more step to the privatization of the corporations.

It should be pointed out that decentralization was needed. Excessive centralization, and the subsequent bureaucratization, was preventing the educational administration from keeping up with scientific and technological progress; economic, social, and demographic development; the political dynamic; and the quantitative and qualitative changes in education itself. Concern over these flaws in the system, particularly among teachers' organizations, began to be voiced during the 1940s, and by the end of the 1950s administrative reform was considered a vital requisite for the integrated planning of education. Diverse factors gave impetus to proposals for reform. The following were particularly important: the growth of political democracy and the demand for full participation by groups that felt left out; the explosive growth in numbers of school-age children; and the diversification of the educational system both in the sense of attention to new needs and objectives (increased number of specialities, degree courses, teaching methods, more-complex activities, etc.) and with regard to geographical extension (more rural elementary education and growing high school education in the small towns throughout the country, regionalization of higher education, etc.). While there was some progress, the various initiatives undertaken did not lead to essential changes in the traditional character of educational administration.[16]

The military government's desire to decentralize was inserted into this context. Although the armed forces came to power in 1973, it was not until 1979–1980 that the main measures regarding education were implemented. The document containing the presidential directives on education of March 1979 did not explicitly mention the transfer of educational administration to the municipalities. It did create a series of commissions and gave them a deadline for implementing the new guidelines. In July of the same year, the report produced by one of the commissions finally formulated the proposal for decentralization. The administrative management of educational establishments for elementary and rural education was to be handed over to a general director or administrator, who would report to a *consejo comunal* (communal council). At the high school level, the director would report to a *consejo de establecimientos* (establishments council).

However, further on the same document proposes that in rural areas, in a first stage, the consejo comunal would not exercise its function of designating directors, determining norms for the distribution of the population of school age, and deciding on the distribution of socioeconomic aid for each school, but that these tasks were to be assumed by the mayor. This model, proposed initially by the commission for rural areas, is the one that served as a basis for the overall municipalization implemented later.

Regarding the financing of education, the commission's proposal suggested a government allowance (corresponding to the government expenditure per pupil) in accordance with the number of pupils registered. (In 1979 government expenditure per elementary school pupil was 455 pesos. For high school students the figure was 698). Nevertheless, the system of subsidies was not considered sufficient, given the growth of educational demand. The number of pupils registered in private schools had stagnated, while the number registered in government schools had grown. The report then suggested that the magnitude of the subsidies should be reexamined and updated in accordance with the new system proposed.

With respect to the working conditions of the staff—that is, teachers— the report suggested that urban elementary and high school teachers be subject to the regime currently in use in the private sector and that the system for teachers in rural areas remain unchanged.

In December 1979 legislation was passed on the transfer of public services to the municipalities. The area of municipal administration has, in turn, undergone various changes. Following Decreto-Ley No. 1289 of January 1976 (Nueva Ley Orgánica de Municipios y Administración Comunal), the municipality was integrated into what was called the "regime of the interior administration of the state" (*el régimen de Administración Interior del Estado*), becoming part of the power structure of the executive and thus an entity that executed policies designed at higher governmental levels. Previous legislation had given the municipality a certain autonomy, even though it was still defined as the local representative of the national government.

In a similar fashion, when municipalization occurred mayors were designated by the president of the Republic, in consultation with the *intendente regional* (regional governor). The 1980 Constitution restricts this faculty in some *comunas* and for the rest gives the responsibility for naming mayors to the Consejos de Desarrollo Regional (Regional Development Councils), following the proposal of the Consejo de Desarrollo Comunal (CODECO, or Community Development Council).[17]

CODECO, which replaced the old Asamblea Comunal, or the group of representatives (*regidores*) who had been elected by democratic vote, is composed of representatives of community organizations that are closely controlled by the executive. Each community organization provides a quarter of the members of CODECO. These organizations are: the Unión Comunal de Juntas de Vecinos (Union of Neighborhood Associations); the Unión Comunal de Centros de Madres (Union of Centers for Mothers); economic activities predominating in the comuna; and heads of municipal divisions (*reparticiones municipales*). While CODECO participates in the elaboration of policies, plans, and programs for communal development, it has no decisionmaking power whatsoever.

In summary, while administrative decentralization progressed at the regional level, through regionalization, the relationship between region and municipality developed a highly centralized character as regional governors became more important in the functioning of the municipalities. It should be remembered that the governors are named by the president.

Citizens' participation is not dealt with, even though the authorities indicate that "the democratic basis of the municipality" rests particularly on their participation. The community is viewed, rather, as receiving the initiatives of the municipality and is expected to support them. In the words of the undersecretary of the interior in August 1980: "the mayor has more than enough faculties to administer the public services that are transferred. The intermediate organizations should, and here we have an important principle of participation, *support* their mayor in the carrying out of this task."[18] This then, is the type of municipality that is to assume the responsibility for public education.

Finally, in June 1980 legislation was passed on the transfer of public services to the municipalities, in the form of DFL 1-3063. And in September of the same year the same decree specified the possibility of transferring municipalized services to private, nonprofit corporations—one step farther on the road to a smaller state, with a smaller role, one step closer to dismantling the welfare state.

A Debate in Progress

The debate as to the size of the state, the type and number of functions it should carry out, is in progress all over the world at present. In Chile the argument appears to be centered on people's dissatisfaction with education. Various national-level surveys indicate that, independently of the political position of the interviewee, the majority prefer that the state be responsible for education and health.[19]

At the level of the teachers themselves, the response is the same or more categorical. Responding to a survey carried out in the Santiago commune, 80 percent of teachers said they favored the state's playing a more active role in education. Eighty-four percent said the state should "administer, supervise, and finance public schools," and supervise the technical, administrative, and pedagogical aspects of both subsidized and fee-charging private education. Almost 100 percent of the interviewees were in favor of public educational establishments run by the state. When asked who should take over the administration of education should decentralization materialize, 49.79 percent said that the state's regional secretariats (*secretarías regionales*) were the appropriate body, 46.05 percent favored other regional authorities (*direcciones regionales*), and only 4.13 percent favored municipalities or private corporations.[20]

Nevertheless, opinions voiced by important spokesmen and practitioners of decentralization are equally vehement. This group says they stand for "the firm defense of an educational system where teaching is carried out without hindrance, thus ruling out any state participation." They also hold that while the political constitution guarantees the right to education, it is not the role of the state to decide where each person should be educated. Freedom of choice exists in this respect.[21] To the teacher is assigned the role of reproducing the regime's ideology. Together with affirming that teachers have "a great effect on the development of the nation, given the responsibility they have in molding the minds of children and young people," it is also noted that in order to fulfil this responsibility it is necessary "to have a clear idea of what the last fifteen years in Chile have meant, especially in economic terms." Now that Chile has been converted into an emergent economic power, the issue is "to maintain the rules of the game" so that the country can become a developed nation by the end of the next decade.[22]

Some of the attacks on the *estado docente* (state-as-educator) have been quite impassioned; for example: "the true prisons of the estado docente had to dispense with their bars and follow the imperative mandate of modern and innovative legislation so that freedom of education and teaching could predominate in our sovereign land, where the dark seeds of educational slavery had flourished."[23]

Such antagonistic visions suggest that the discussion will continue. What is clear is that there are signs of a crisis, reflected in the state of education and in the living and working conditions of teachers. With regard to the former, two systems of evaluation have been applied. It is notorious that the results of the Programa de Evaluación del Rendimiento (Program for Evaluating Educational Results), implemented for the last time in 1983, were never published and were finally shelved. It became known, however, that the results were very unsatisfactory. A second system was then implemented, the Sistema de Medición de la Calidad de la Educación (SIMCE; or System for Measuring the Quality of Education), whose results were published in 1989. These studies revealed that in none of the subjects evaluated were more than 57 percent of the proposed objectives achieved: Spanish, 54.22 percent; mathematics, 51.81; natural science, 53.23; and social science, 56.78 percent.[24] The methodology also showed the differences between the results obtained in the private fee-charging schools—the best—and the municipal schools—the worst. In mathematics, for example, the respective percentages of achieved objectives were 73.9 and 58.5 percent.[25]

Dissatisfaction is very high with regard to the living conditions of teachers, as we will see. The many letters from teachers to the press indicate how unhappy they are with their lot.

> Why do teachers always get only crumbs? I will give an example. On the large island of Chiloé, various teachers had their homes in Castro (eighteen or twenty kilometers from the provincial capital). If their salaries oscillate between 25,000 and 50,000 pesos a month and they spend 10,000 or 15,000 on transport and food, and if we consider that most are heads of families or have to rent accommodation in the city, any reader can see the economic anxiety in which they live.
>
> The same bitterness is suffered by thousands and thousands of colleagues throughout the country. Nobody with his heart in the right place could call this a political, ideological, or political party "problem." It is a question of minimal decent and necessary human subsistence, in accordance with the level of education and the social role of the teaching profession, which are not taken fully into account by the current government.
>
> In order to alleviate this unjust and miserable situation, here in Chiloé some teachers go out deep-sea fishing during the holiday period, risking their lives to increment the paltry income society gives them.
>
> Who cares about this improper sacrifice on the part of the teachers?
>
> How is it that the growing protests of teachers are held in such contempt, and then the same teachers are praised with such flowery speeches celebrating the Día del Maestro [Teachers' Day], the Semana del Niño [Childhood Week], and at the beginning and end of the school year?
>
> Many of us await urgent economic just solutions.
> —Fernando Mario Oyarzún Gómez, Castro[26]

Another frustrated citizen wrote:

> On Saturday the first of July your prestigious newspaper published an advertisement that read: "Home help needed. I offer 35,000 pesos, plus taxes." A full-time state teacher (thirty hours) earns 3,000 pesos more than the domestic servant. These are the facts; I have no wish to make any further comment so as to let the information speak for itself."
> —Fernando C. de I. 6.267.151-3, Santiago[27]

The question should be raised as to whether the poor results obtained when education is evaluated and the deficient living conditions of the teachers are not closely linked.

Finally, teachers' generalized discontent was seen in the elections for the board of the Colegio de Profesores, when 70 percent of the votes favored those who opposed the military government. As we pointed out at the beginning of this chapter, the president of the association, reelected in June 1989, centered his campaign discourse on the need to revalidate the state's role in education, teachers' participation in the design of educational policy, and the recovery of dignity for the teacher. In summary, all the evidence seems to indicate that the Chilean teacher, traditionally appointed by the state administration and thus a public employee, resists being "privatized," at least when the political conditions of the country allow him to express his opinion on the matter.

The efficiency of the neoliberal model, applied in Chile without the possibility of protest, is based on the assumption that the market is the best mechanism for assigning resources. Conditions for free competition must thus be created, which will permit the triumph of "the best" (the most efficient). Teachers have entered into this free market and are expected to compete. In the transition to the private sector, they have suffered a series of losses that we have described above, but whose consequences in terms of the lives of teachers, as real, flesh-and-blood people, will be explored in the next chapter.

Notes

1. *El Mercurio* (Santiago), May 7, 1989.
2. Programa Interdisciplinario de Investigaciones en Educación (PIIE), *Las transformaciones educacionales bajo el régimen militar*, vol. 1, ch. 4: "El magisterio y la política educacional."
3. Ibid., p. 152.
4. Ibid., pp. 154–155.
5. See *La Epoca* (Santiago), April 18, 1989. There is a Comisión Nacional de Profesores Exonerados (national commission of exonerated teachers), headed by José Galaz. According to Galaz, since 1973 a total of 25,000 teachers have been dismissed.
6. Navarro, *Diagnóstico de la realidad educacional chilena*, pp. 30–31; PIIE, "El magisterio y la política educacional," pp. 156–158. See also n. 5, above.
7. PIIE, "El magisterio y la política educacional," p. 157.
8. Ibid., pp. 182–184; Navarro, "Diagnóstico de la realidad educacional chilena."
9. CIEPLAN, "Balance económico-social del régimen militar," in Tironi, *Los silencios de la revolución*.
10. Ibid., pp. 169–173.
11. PIIE ibid., p. 175.
12. Historian Sergio Villalobos, quoted in *La Epoca* (Santiago), May 5, 1989.
13. PIIE, "El magisterio y la política educacional," p. 123.
14. *La Epoca* (Santiago), January 17, 1989.
15. Sergio Soto, leader of the Colegio de Profesores, in a statement published in *La Epoca* (Santiago), January 17, 1989.
16. PIIE, "El magisterio y la política educacional," pp. 116–119.
17. This ruling has been impugned by the political opposition, which demands the reinstatement of the community's right to elect its own local government and mayor, except in certain cases traditionally proscribed by the law.
18. Montero, *Traspaso de servicios publicos a la municipalidades*, quoted in PIIE, "El magisterio y la política educacional," p. 127 (emphasis added).

19. Centro de Estudios Públicos (CED), "Estudio social y de opinión pública en la población de Santiago."
20. *La Epoca* (Santiago), May 7, 1989.
21. *El Mercurio* (Santiago), March 19, 1989. This commentary refers to a meeting of the board of the Centro Democrático Libre (CDL, Free Democratic Center)—Luis Danús, Alvaro Bardón, Hugo Galassi, and Pilar Velasco—with representatives of the teaching profession in Santiago.
22. Alvaro Vial, director of the Instituto Nacional de Estadística (INE), in *El Mercurio* (Santiago), May 7, 1989.
23. Mónica Madariaga, ex-minister of education for the military regime, in *La Epoca* (Santiago), May 13, 1989.
24. *La Epoca* (Santiago), July 26, 1989.
25. *La Epoca* (Santiago), August 7, 1989.
26. *La Epoca* (Santiago), May 17, 1989.
27. *El Mercurio* (Santiago), July 9, 1989.

5

The Teachers

We worked with fifteen informants in this study, all of them teachers, some of them men and some women, of varying ages, backgrounds, and training. Their occupational biographies are different, and so are the solutions they have sought to the problem of survival.

In no sense is this group a representative sample of the total universe of teachers. Despite the variety, however, the study of their biographies reveals coincidences that allow us to sketch out a sort of collective biography:

- the social origin and self-evaluation of the informant
- the vision and appreciation of the function of education
- the deterioration of living and working conditions, with the subsequent difficulty in preserving social status
- the use of social capital (social networks)

Nevertheless, these biographies, obtained by means of interviews and participant observation, also revealed a factor of differentiation. The older informants, a group of four—two women and two men, all around sixty years old—had been particularly affected by the military takeover in 1973.

We have divided the presentation of this case study into three parts: the first deals with the older teachers; the second with what we have called the collective biography; and finally, we have selected five cases and let them speak for themselves in extenso.

The Older Teachers

In 1973 Graciela Berríos, Rosario Vásquez, Ignacio Narbona, and Ernesto Maldonado had all found a path in life. They were all about forty-five years old and worked happily in their posts in the educational sector. Graciela Berríos and Rosario Vásquez taught in prestigious high schools. Graciela taught mathematics, and Rosario, French. Ignacio Narbona and Ernesto Maldonado worked in different departments of the Ministerio de Educación. They had achieved their positions on the basis of their knowledge or research in the area of pedagogy. Furthermore, Ignacio gave classes in the Instituto Pedagógico, the Universidad de Chile's department of education.

The military coup changed their lives abruptly. While they were not all political militants, they were committed to the political and social process initiated by the Unidad Popular government, and this meant their immediate dismissal. Ernesto left without resigning but applied for unpaid leave. The others were given the sack ("exonerated"). "I had worked in my school for twelve years," said Graciela, "and I was fired on November 12, 1973, with a note that said 'you are relieved of your post by order of the authorities.' We were made to read a document that prohibited us from going anywhere near the offices of the Ministerio de Educación or returning to the school. When I asked why, I was told to obey 'the orders of the authorities [*órdenes superiores*].'"

Something similar happened to Rosario Vásquez. Both teachers repeatedly appealed against these measures until they were allowed to go back to teaching in public schools, but not in the schools they had worked in before. Both of them tell of the harassment and humiliations they were subjected to in their new jobs. This situation was dealt with differently by the two teachers. Rosario continued in the system, even though she was not at all happy: "I should be retired by now. I have completed thirty years of service. I began working at a very young age and have worked for forty years. I would like to retire but my income would drop considerably. They asked me to retire two years ago, but I have tried to carry on. Now, the job instability and the daily uncertainties mean that one works with no enthusiasm or involvement. However, I do like my work, I feel I'm still of some use, I feel I've got something to offer the young, and I always try to keep up to date."

Meanwhile, Graciela Berríos at first tried to stay on in the publicly run high school system, but, "they sent me to a high school where I just could not stay on. I really couldn't stand it. I was watched, for example. Sometimes while I was teaching my class, an inspector would patrol the classroom. Or else I would suddenly see him on the balcony in front of the window. He would come in and interrupt what I was saying. . . . Soon, they gave me some courses in classrooms in a place they called Siberia because it was very damp. The floors were damp . . . they were makeshift classrooms really. Well, I gave my classes there and ended up with pneumonia, and the truth is that I never went back. I couldn't do it. They won that round."

Finally, she found a job teaching mathematics in a prestigious private school. However, like Rosario, she was not happy. "This situation produces a conflict in me because I have really always felt that my work is with the children in public schools, the children from low-income homes. I wanted these children to have a chance to have good teachers and decent schooling. . . . So, when I find myself in this private school teaching rich kids, I feel angry. I feel I'm not doing my job, that this isn't what I'm supposed to do. I make excuses for myself sometimes, saying that I taught in government schools for twenty-seven years, but I am only deceiving myself. It makes no real difference to my feelings how long I was in public schools. . . . But now, a pensioner, I have no chance at all of getting into a government-run high school, not even with only ten hours' teaching a week. They just won't have me."

Ignacio Narbona lost his job in the Ministerio de Educación and was relieved of his post in the Universidad de Chile. "I lost my classes and all the accumulated years of work in the institute—my seniority. I was expelled after a sort of indictment. This happened to the majority of the teachers in the institute. It was very painful, a terrible blow, because it wasn't just a simple dismissal . . . we were indicted . . . the charges were handed out to us as mimeographed copies, a standard charge for everyone, so vague you couldn't even begin to try to answer it. In other words, you felt the victim of a trick, of a machine—much worse than just being told 'don't come back.'"

In spite of the fact that his post in the ministry had been political (in the sense that he was appointed personally by the president), Ignacio did obtain a pension, since there was a ruling to that effect covering precisely his type of case. Thus, he could at least cover his basic necessities of life. "This pension has been adjusted to a certain extent so that today I receive about 50,000 pesos net [about US $200]. At the time it meant that we did not suffer too much, although of course our income fell, but we never got to the stage of not having enough to get by on."

Ignacio's wife, also a teacher employed in the Ministerio de Educación, did not lose her job but was transferred to another department. "She survived there until 1978, if I'm not mistaken, until she had completed twenty-five years of service. That's when they allow women to retire. All that time she was pushed into a corner, discriminated against, watched, but they let her stay. It was very painful, very difficult for her."

In the meantime, Ignacio was invited to collaborate with a nongovernmental organization as a researcher working from his home. "The director offered me a marvelous opportunity, which was very significant at that time: to work for the center from my home. . . . I took a whole lot of documents home with me, worked on them, and then either my wife or I took them back in to the center. Of course, they didn't pay me much but—given the situation of insecurity and anxiety—it helped me keep my mind occupied in an area I enjoyed working in because it was close to what I had done previously." This work, carried out in semiclandestine conditions, allowed Ignacio to keep himself up to date, and, in his own words, "I learned a lot and read the latest in the field. In actual fact I was almost doing a postgraduate course."

Suddenly, and in spite of his "clandestine existence," Ignacio was arrested. "Being detained had nothing to do with what I had been. They didn't come after me for that reason. In fact, I was innocent of the concrete reason for my arrest." A person who wanted to have an interview with Ignacio Narbona had also been arrested. This person was followed, detained, and then tortured. It was while he was under torture that he had said he wanted to make contact with Narbona. Ignacio explained: "so I was arrested and they started to interrogate me about this man, whom I didn't actually know. In all honesty, I did not know him. Since I replied that I knew nothing, they tortured me until they realized that effectively I knew nothing. I think they realized it because in fact the torture . . . it was only one day of torture . . . of course, one day of torture but nine more days in the detention center of the DINA [Dirección Nacional de Inteligencia], which is like being tortured mentally. When we were not alone in between interrogations, we were all kept in collective cells; they were always coming for somebody, and then you would see the state they returned in, hear the screams, and you never knew when it was going to be your turn again."

After being forced to sign a document, Ignacio was sent to the concentration camps Three and Four Alamos until he was freed, together with a large number of other prisoners. Although exile was not obligatory, many opted to leave the country. Narbona also played with the idea but finally stayed on. An ex-teacher offered him the opportunity of doing the Chilean part of a Latin American research project. The project leader turned out to be a Chilean woman who had been one of his teachers, and he accepted the offer with pleasure. Finally, he was hired (with tenure) by another nongovernmental organization where he could continue to do his research.

Ernesto Maldonado's story is similar to Ignacio's in that he also kept well out of sight after leaving the ministry. At first, he was confirmed in his post. "I carried on in the ministry, but in practice I was not allowed to do anything. I was removed from all the projects I had directed . . . and then I had nothing to do. I was like an old piece of furniture, getting paid at the end of the month. I was even accused of sabotage, of destroying the lavatories. . . . I realized that they were closing in on me and so . . . since they had sacked an enormous number of university professors, the left-wing professors, there was a lot of work available. . . . I said to my wife, 'I'm going to apply for one of those jobs,' which I did, in a provincial town where I had family."

Ernesto got the job and did not tell anyone in the ministry where he had gone. He moved his family to a nearby town and began to work in the university. He even managed to carry out a piece of research on the situation of teachers at all levels of the educational system in the area. Later, under pressure from Santiago, he returned to the ministry to resign his post there. "From there I went to the center of Santiago, to the Universidad de Chile where I found the vice-rector of my campus, with all the other vice-rectors, looking anything but happy. I told him I had just resigned from the ministry . . . and he replied telling me they had just done away with the campus where I worked."

Faced with this and then further periods of unemployment, Maldonado showed himself to be extremely resourceful. He always had an idea up his sleeve and even "invented" jobs for himself, although they did not always last long. He gave a few hours of classes and earned very little. "My family continued to live in the provinces. We lived on a minimal amount of money. . . . My wife began to sell books and other things to see if that could earn us enough to eat.".

With a few hours of teaching in the South, Ernesto also managed to get some teaching work in a university in Santiago. He traveled back and forth between the two. "My income from the two universities was really miserable. At the time it must have been the equivalent of 15,000 pesos today [around US $80], at the very most." A friend with a large unoccupied house lent him a room so he did not have to pay rent. "I ate bread, sometimes not much else, and I had to save money for the train journey. Later I managed to get a discount on the train tickets. And the university there [in the South] gave me a small room and food."

At this point, Maldonado began to think about leaving the country, an economic exile. But after being rejected on the grounds of age, number of dependents, and type of profession (teachers were not in demand), he abandoned the idea and once again began to create things—a cultural center; a project for a corporation offering courses outside the conventional educational institutions—and at the same time he got a master's degree in education from the Universidad Católica. When he gave the details of his case he was exempted from paying tuition.

Through an old acquaintance, a foreigner, he got some support from an international organization for a study of the basic educational needs of a marginal area of Santiago, with a view to getting some background information for his educational project. He got together a team of colleagues and interviewers, and after selecting a group from a shantytown (who were "scared to death"), he began to structure a participatory study. However, his economic situation did not improve. The monetary aid the project received served only to pay his colleagues. He continued to live on what he earned by his university teaching. "I was interested in how this would work out. It was pretty underground and fraught with anxiety. The methodology developed was quite new for those times . . . and in the conclusions, the inhabitants of the area said they wanted a school, but one with special characteristics."

The proposal for this special school was sent abroad and found funding to the tune of US $40,000. It began with two teachers. In the meantime, Maldonado resigned from the southern university. An acquaintance had told him about the chance of some hours of counseling work at a night school. He got the job, "then things got a little better for me, but only a very little. Afterward, when they introduced the Carrera Docente, with great difficulty I managed to get my hours turned into a proper job—my eight hours became a post of counselor, with a much improved income." So Ernesto could then bring his family to Santiago, to live in the same big old house where his friend had given him refuge. Even so, the family did not have enough to live on, and his wife began to take in students from the provinces as paying guests—the companions of their own children.

The special school was created as a subsidized private school. Maldonado appointed a director, and it still functions today with 450 pupils (it began with forty). As president of the corporation running the school, Maldonado receives no income. He still presents projects to the same agency that helped him in the first instance, and to others as well. He directs another school, supported by an industrial union, which pertains to the same corporation. "You have to create spaces," says Ernesto.

Of these four cases of older teachers (and also of all the teachers we interviewed), Maldonado was the only one to have "privatized," using the rules of the system to his own ends. Without giving up his belief in the estado docente, or his progressive vision of the educational process, he is the only one to be involved in the current educational system from "the other side"; that is, he is the "boss" and not a salaried worker.

The notion of "creating spaces" for yourself or others is directly linked to the situation of dictatorship in the country. The expression appears frequently and is used indiscriminately at the personal or political level. As a result, the separation between creating space for yourself (the search for a personal solution) and creating spaces (the search for a collective solution) is by no means categorical. While it is true that nongovernmental organizations, for example, have created collective spaces, they arose promoted by people who also had a personal problem of survival to solve. But at the same time, their motives went beyond personal concerns in the sense that they aimed at opening up opportunities for the expression of an unofficial ideology, an ideology of protest. Other institutions, such as the Vicaría de la Solidaridad, as well as trying to solve the specific problems derived from the persecution of many Chileans, opened up spaces to people who wanted to do something precisely to find solutions to such problems. To create spaces also included the idea of opening up channels for the free expression of ideas, to maintain or to create mass media that could air opposition views. Politically, opposition initiatives gradually did create spaces; the government was forced to accept alternative or critical positions.

Without pretending to have exhausted the theme, we have tried to explain something of the reasons for the appearance of the expression *create spaces,* which has so often been commented on by foreign observers of Chilean reality.

To sum up the case of the older teachers, none of the four we spoke to left the country, despite having suffered a certain amount of political persecution as a result of their left-wing activities, which, after the military coup, passed from being something quite normal in Chile to being a crime. Nevertheless, they all remained involved in education. The two women returned to the classroom after an arduous bureaucratic struggle (although one of them had to work in a private school). The two men gradually got back into pedagogical research or teaching by means of the alternative channels that they themselves created.

A Collective Biography

While not all our informants came from families in which other members were teachers, most of them had at least one relative who was—a parent, a brother, uncles, et cetera. Four of the cases did come from families of teachers, with three or more teachers in each instance. In only three cases were there no other teachers, either in the past or the present. Two of these latter cases were rather more prosperous families.

The case of Irma Gómez merits a separate mention. She describes her family as "impoverished gentry." "My parents never owned property or anything like that. But their world and their surnames . . . the world that surrounded them was culturally aristocratic, and the families all had well-known names. I studied in a convent run by nuns. At the time, my family's cultural milieu was the best there was in Santiago. But in economic terms, it was another story. We never had anything at home, we always had scholarships at school, always. There was never money for anything at all."

The rest of our informants came from low-income families (in cultural terms as well, these families were not well endowed). Some of them had known serious economic difficulties, and the majority were from the provinces or of peasant stock, poor or destitute. In these cases, for their parents or for the informants themselves, access to the teaching profession was a means of social mobility. Santiago Peralta said: "My grandparents' family was . . . I remember as a child up until I was eleven, we had a comfortable life. We had a lot of things, we owned mines, farmland, and other things. But we were a family of gamblers, and a lot of the children turned out quite wild (my father was one) and squandered the family money. My father didn't finish school in the North because he got married. . . . Well, I remember when I was eleven we lost the farm, for example. Everything had to be sold . . . and then, well, our economic situation was never the same again."

Except for the cases where one of the parents is or was a teacher, in only three cases did we find parents in the liberal professions—lawyers, accountants. In one case only the father was in the armed forces. In the rest the parents exercised a variety of often vaguely defined activities such as bank employee, bus driver, public employee, salesman.

Despite clearly belonging to the middle class, all our informants, with two exceptions, studied for their professional qualifications in the midst of great monetary difficulties, and could only do so thanks to the free tuition (we will discuss this further in the section on professional training).

In two cases the informants referred to their childhood in terms of the quality of the teacher in the family, the father in one case and the mother in the other. "It's in our blood," said Sonia Salas, and added: "When I was three I spent the whole day in a school. We crossed the street, a dirt road actually because we lived in the country, and there was the school. I played all day in my mother's classroom, behind her seat."

Ignacio Narbona's father was a teacher and school principal. "For two or three years we lived in a house away from the school in a working-class district. Later we went to live in the school itself when the new school buildings were put up, the modern school, erected by the Sociedad Constructora de Establecimientos Educacionales. There was a house for the principal in the new school. From then on I lived the life of the school intensely, I was more than just a pupil, I felt a bit as if I owned the place. When I stayed on in the vacations, it was as if I owned the building. You have to try to imagine what an enormous building like a new school was for a child . . . there were workshops for manual activities, a library, it had an enormous gymnasium. There was a terrace on top from which you could watch the city. My school was my world. And from the more human perspective, there was also the extraordinary experience of being with the group of teachers and my father, the social and cultural life of all the teachers there. . . . Even as the child that I was, I learned a lot about what the teaching profession is. I knew what a class attendance book was, how it was filled in; I saw my father writing the annual report or doing some practical activity—he told me this himself—I learned to use a typewriter. The tasks he had to carry out were very familiar to me."

Becoming a Teacher

Studying the history of the training of our informants as teachers gives the general impression of a long process, sometimes plagued with difficulties. In only one of our cases, that of Alvaro Canales, the goal was not achieved, for political reasons (the complete history of this teacher is found farther on). Except in the case of Santiago Peralta, who, as a result of coming from a family that moved around the country a lot, attended twelve schools in the thirteen years of his elementary and high school education, the rest all got through their preuniversity education without too much difficulty.

In three cases, those of Irma Gómez, Juana Barros, and Marcia Vidal, the informants began their schooling in private schools, but Marcia Vidal—because of family economic difficulties—completed her studies in a publicly run high school (*liceo fiscal*). All the rest studied in publicly run schools. Only one informant, from the provinces, entered the Escuela Normal (Teacher-Training College) in his hometown.

The story of how they qualified as teachers is much more complex. As is common in Chile, they all began working before graduating. In some cases the path followed was anything but conventional—that is, elementary school, high school, university. Let us look at Santiago Peralta, for example. "I had to repeat the third year of high school and decided to work during the day and study the third and fourth years at night school. Then I entered the Seminario Mayor in Santiago. I wanted to be a priest and graduate in philosophy. In August 1973 I left the seminary . . . and went north. Well, then there was the coup, and things got very complicated up there. . . . I came back to Santiago. My mother [a teacher] was working in a private school. One of the teachers resigned . . . around November. Since there was only a replacement teacher available for a month, my mother spoke to the principal and told her she had a son who had studied philosophy who perhaps could . . . and I started working there on a temporary basis; then they paid me my vacations too, and I started working without being qualified. In March I took my exams again (I had taken them before) and got a post in the area of English teaching."

Félix Briones, another of our informants, taught for a time in the Escuela de Carabineros (Police Academy), at his father's wish. Then he left and began to study mechanical engineering in the provinces. He did not like the subject and returned to Santiago. With the help of a friend he got a job in a government office and then started studying in the Escuela Normal in Santiago. "The coup got me before I finished college, when I was doing teaching practice in Pudahuel. The Escuela Normal had agreements with some of the school districts in Santiago, and as a result the students were sent out to certain schools for teaching practice. These were usually schools without enough teachers and so we filled the need by doing our teaching practice there."

When the college was closed down, the students who had not finished their studies were assimilated by the various universities. "I managed to finish in the Pedagógico," Briones recalled. "Some of my previous studies in the area of humanities were recognized (except in social sciences where I had to do the courses all over again), and I qualified as a high school physical education teacher."

Sonia Salas, whose biography we have included in full farther on, calls her experience "the longest undergraduate education in history," on account of the many years it took her to qualify.

In contrast, Ernesto Maldonado has three degrees—as a teacher of history, a counselor, and also a master of education.

Our youngest informant, Marcia Vidal, was the only one to have studied in an *instituto profesional.* All the rest graduated from either the Universidad de Chile or the Universidad Católica. Vidal's personal view of her lack of a university education was that it was a definite drawback when applying for jobs. "In my experience, at least, when you are interviewed for a job it is a disadvantage to have studied in a private institute; there's always this feeling that the university . . . " Nevertheless, she feels that this a priori judgment is unjust, since she says "you get to know people who have studied in different places and can compare their work . . . and then you can see that really the efficiency and quality [of the others] is a lot lower."

In most cases, financing their studies was not a major problem for our informants, since they studied during a period in which the university was free (the Universidad de Chile) or else there was a system of scholarships and other means of making payment of tuition accessible (the Universidad Católica). Only one of the informants, Fernando Morales, studied in the Universidad Católica with a government grant, which he is still paying off and which is a heavy burden, given his small income. Morales left university in 1980 and, like all the others, began working before graduating and before beginning to pay off his loan. In 1986, when he wanted to finish his studies in order to be able to qualify, he found that he could not graduate before he had put his loan repayments in order. "I took my exams and everything went fine. But when I went to get my degree certificate, they told me I had to pay back what I owed first. By that time, with the added interest payments and other adjustments, I found I owed a monstrous amount." (Morales's case is also included in detail below.) According to data provided by the Colegio de Profesores, of a total of approximately ninety thousand young teachers, thirty-five thousand are behind with their repayments on university loans.

The current cost of a university education worries most of our informants in relation to their own children. The conditions they live in now make them fear that their children may not be able to acquire the status they have achieved and now have to struggle to maintain.

Living and Working Conditions

> *I will never forget an elementary teacher, thin, hungry— the man was probably also ill. He spoke very badly, probably as a result of his bad health. He came to offer his services at this school. Look, I tell you, I'll never forget that face because it is the face of the teaching profession in Chile today.* —an informant

As we have said, all the teachers we interviewed began teaching before graduating. This is not a new phenomenon; it was as common among the older teachers as it was among the younger ones. The widespread nature of this practice could be clearly observed in 1987, when the reason given for the massive dismissal of teachers was that they had not graduated, despite the fact they had been teaching for years.

Almost all the people we studied finally graduated and continued to teach. There was one exception, and he had to start out in a different field. Those who entered government teaching establishments followed a common pattern, accepting "a few hours of classes" at first and finally obtaining a permanent post (*la planta*). Others went straight into subsidized private schools, and only two worked in private fee-charging schools, of great prestige. These two were Graciela Berríos, who we mentioned earlier, and Irma Gómez, of upper-class extraction.

However, Irma's occupational history was not without its problems. She began working in 1973 and was employed in a series of subsidized private schools, until she was hired by a private school charging no fees—in a low-income area—operated by a prestigious college run by priests. Later, in 1984, this school closed, and Irma Gómez started teaching in another private school where she felt overwhelmed by the amount of work. Finally, in 1986 she was invited to join a school run by priests, as an elementary teacher. According to her own view of her story, her economic situation up till this moment had been bad; today she considers herself fortunate to earn a net income of 90,000 pesos (over US $300) for forty-two hours of work, of which twenty-one are class hours—that is, hours spent in the classroom.

This means that she has the time to work in a department of the Colegio de Profesores as well, where she is involved in the training of workshop leaders. Gómez is separated from her husband and has a son thirteen years old. Since she got married she has been the family breadwinner. She lives in her own apartment that she bought with the severance pay she received when the school in the poor neighborhood closed; she pays a 15,000 peso mortgage. Since she separated from her husband, she has shared the apartment, first with a colleague, then with her brother and his family. Later she shared with a female friend and another colleague with a son. Now she shares with her sister and her sister's two children.

Nearly all the informants have two jobs. They either work in two schools or else give private classes (as Graciela Berríos does), work in the vacations teaching sports (Félix Briones), give courses for the improvement of certain skills (Marcia Vidal, Sonia Salas, and Pedro Guzmán), or do something completely divorced from teaching, as in the extreme case of Fernando Morales, who is a salesman for a pension scheme.

Morales had a car accident that left him with a large debt. He started as a salesman in order to be able to pay what he owed. With his salary and that of his wife he would never have been able to do so, even though his wife, also a teacher, has two jobs, one in an elementary school and another in a subsidized private school. Between the two of them they have a net income of about 100,000 pesos (about US $350). They pay 20,000 pesos in rent and spend about 35,000 pesos on food; electricity, water, gas for cooking and heating, and telephone account for 10,000 pesos; the maid receives 15,000; the elder child's kindergarten costs 10,000; and then, "if there is anything left over—gasoline, for the car."

Up until August 1988 Fernando taught in two schools and dedicated himself entirely to teaching. The car accident forced him to look for an additional occupation, one that paid more money, since his income was no longer sufficient. "Either for saving or for an emergency . . . not a cent of what my wife and I earn can be put aside without depriving Fernanda of her kindergarten, or eating less, neither of which are we willing to do."

Marcia Vidal began teaching as a temporary in an Adventist school but had to leave because she did not share the school's religious beliefs. She then managed to get thirty hours at a subsidized private school, where they paid her 15,000 pesos in 1987. During the 1988 summer vacation she worked in the Summer School of the Colegio de Profesores. There she made a contact that enabled her to get her current job in a private school, offering "alternative" education, where she earns 30,000 pesos for twenty-five hours a week. The rest of her time she uses for research and improving her professional skills.

Marcia is a single woman living in her own apartment. Her father pays the mortgage. In exchange, she maintains a cousin from the provinces who is studying in Santiago. When she became "independent" of her family by going to live on her own, she made a promise to save 5,000 pesos a month (about US $20) in order to be able to finance future studies, but "the 5,000 pesos I promised to save is too much because it is a very large part of the 30,000 I earn. I spend about 6,000 pesos on food a week. I buy vegetables in the market and spend between 2,000 and 3,000 pesos a week there. Electricity, water, and other utilities come to about 7,000 pesos. It all adds up." One of her main expenses is transportation, which she calculates at around 8,000 pesos a month.

On the subject of women in education, Marcia says: "In Chile 70 percent of teachers are women . . . the fact is that male teachers can't afford a house, children, et cetera, unless their wife works or they have very good jobs. Usually they choose other work or else do additional work that isn't teaching. I know what it's like because my boyfriend is a teacher too, and right now he is trying to study something different. He was married and got separated, largely for economic reasons; they were both teachers and they simply couldn't manage; it got to the point where they didn't even have the bus fare to get to work."

Félix Briones started out with seven hours in a school in San Miguel. Later, thanks to a friend, he managed to complete a schedule of thirty-six hours in a school on the other side of the city. He felt the situation was ideal, since he earned between 35,000 and 40,000 pesos and filled his schedule working a half day. Furthermore, since he was a physical education teacher, he got an additional job in a company where they paid him "well," until the firm went bankrupt.

When the Carrera Docente was established, Briones's schedule was concentrated in one of the schools. He then got a job in a subsidized private school where he earned 30 percent less than in the government-run school. He stayed only a year in the private school, as they wanted him to work full-time and he preferred to keep his post in the public school. He asked to be transferred to the area (comuna) where he lived, where he now earns 35,000 pesos in a high school. His wife went on working, but all the same their income was insufficient. Through a friend she got a job in a church school.

Today, with fifty-five hours of classes, she earns 83,000 pesos. She works from eight o'clock in the morning until seven o'clock at night, every day including Saturday.

Félix experienced the municipalization of his school. "It was a public school. We went from the municipality to the private corporation. The process was accompanied by the loss of a series of rights; for example, job stability, a basic issue. Previously an indictment was the only cause for dismissal. Today it has all been lost; seniority has been lost, and *la perseguidora* [this is a pension given to the higher ranks of the civil service, which keeps up with the current salary of the category]." "If you are fired," added Briones, "you get paid one month for every year you have worked." Since he has been two years in the municipal corporation, he would get two months' pay if he were sacked. "It's terrible, really terrible, because now job instability means that a teacher has to humiliate himself in order to keep his job. He has to do what he is told, and if you behave otherwise they accuse you of being a Marxist or of being incompetent, and in the long run you'll be the first to go."

The majority of our informants evaluated the municipalization of education negatively. They pointed to the fact that it put the teachers at the mercy of the labor market and subjected them to the laws of the Plan Laboral, which leaves the worker with few opportunities for protest after, for example, being fired. Rosario Vásquez commented: "The crisis in education came when it was turned into a business, and other values became the important ones. Each school receives a subsidy per pupil, so the concern is to maintain the pupil whatever the cost. There was a major crisis two years ago, a large number of teachers were thrown out of their jobs and lost all their rights. I have colleagues with seventeen years of service who had no chance of retiring with some sort of pension or of recovering their social security payments, unless they agreed to pay for another twenty years more."

In Fernando Morales's opinion, "the main problem for the teachers who lost their jobs was municipalization. A large number of the schools that are now municipally run had been run by the federal government before. All education was transferred to the municipalities, and, as a result, from a technical and administrative point of view, the schools are dependent on the municipalities and function with a subsidy just like any private subsidized school."

Marcia Vidal said: "there are forty-five pupils per classroom; we are required by the mayor to attend innumerable events of all sorts; we have to do everything they say; the principal has no academic degree. The principals of the municipal schools don't have to be teachers. Neither do the principals of the subsidized schools. The owner *[sostenedor]* is the principal." "So," Félix Briones asked, "what does the sostenedor do, the owner of the school? He gives preference to the pupils rather than to the teachers, when it used to be the other way around: first there was the professional and then the student.

Why the change? Because the student means income and the teacher means expenditure; the child gives money to the owner and the teacher takes money from him."

Yet Briones considers his family fortunate. He and his wife together earn about 170,000 pesos. "In this sense we are very privileged; I can see there are many people who haven't enough to eat. Next to them we're almost rich, but from my point of view we have a minimum." Briones lives in his own house, paying a 16,000 peso mortgage. "We were about five years without paying anything; first we fell behind a month. If you fail to pay one month it's because you just can't manage. Then the following month, well, if you can't pay one, it's not likely you'll be able to pay two . . . and so it went on until the moment came when we couldn't pay at all. They were asking a lot just to start talking about it so we decided to leave things as they were and see what happened. Then a new policy was announced, not long ago [as a result of the approaching plebiscite], that aimed at finding a solution. In our case part of the payments we had failed to make was passed to the end of the amortization program, and we could pick up paying the mortgage again, and we have been doing this to this day."

For Briones, the house and the children are his priorities regarding expenditure. Since he and his wife both work, they need a servant. The lack of a maid complicates their lives enormously. He explains that having been without someone to help look after the children for a long time has given him an ulcer—"all the running about because we didn't have anyone to leave the children with. Sometimes my wife or myself had to take them to school or the office. You just can't function properly like that."

Briones, with work in two schools and a wife with work as well, thinks of himself as privileged. And so he is in relation to those earning 30,000, 40,000, or 50,000 pesos, like Santiago Peralta, who earns 56,000 pesos and has four dependents; or compared with Sonia Salas, one of our informants who is practically unemployed.

Salas's occupational history began with a temporary replacement job in an elementary school, before she had any specialized training at all. She had just graduated from high school. While she studied philosophy in the university, she earned money in an assortment of ways, like selling things, working in a bookshop, and making handicrafts. She is separated from her husband; they have three children. In 1974 she got a job of seventeen hours teaching in a township near Santiago in a government-run school attended by one of her sons. She earned very little and survived thanks to help from her ex-husband. Today the money she receives from the children's father, a fixed quantity originating from an inheritance, amounts to 10,500 pesos.

At one point she fell ill and had to take a year's leave of absence. She did receive some sort of social security payments during this period. When she returned to work the Ministerio de Educación divided her work load between two different schools, which she found very hard going. "So I went to another high school where I could work full-time in the one place, thinking it would be better. But the new criteria were employed. Municipalization was on the way, and the economic criteria dictated that heads had to roll. So teachers were sacked, transferred, et cetera, et cetera. Of course, I had been the last to arrive and so I was the first to be transferred. I found myself constantly on the move, as I was always the last to arrive and subsequently the first to leave. So I changed from one school to another and ended up in a commercial college."

There were a succession of changes there, too, as the work load was divided up. Finally, Sonia got a job in a government-run school near her home. Then the municipalization process began, and, because she had participated in strikes protesting the measure, she was fired in 1987. She managed to get a job in a high school, paying 45,000 pesos, and "with one thing and another I earned about 20,000 pesos more." Together with the 10,500 from her ex-husband, this was her income during 1987. During that year, however, she changed jobs several times for different reasons (the detailed biography of Sonia Salas can be found farther on).

Today, she teaches a variety of courses—expression; counseling; skill improvement (workshops sponsored by the Colegio de Profesores)—and lives precariously with her three children, practicing what she calls "economic gymnastics." "I have so many debts. I owe eighteen months of school fees. I have just been told they will cut off my water supply if I don't pay up. I owe the telephone, too, and it could be cut off any time. I am up to date with the rent; I have to be because of the legal problems I've had here." (Sonia was to be thrown out of the apartment for failing to pay the rent in the past.) This is why the 30,000 pesos she earns at an institute, counseling and working in the area of psychological learning difficulties, is used to pay the rent.

When Sonia was asked what she was going to do about this situation, she answered: "invent something new." "Invent something new" is the equivalent of the "create a space for yourself" we talked about before. But not the teachers are able to invent something new; they just live out their situation, worried by the instability, angry at their own impotence, getting by economically as best they can, working too hard but holding on tight to their profession. In this effort to survive as teachers, contacts, acquaintances, and the family all play an important role, as we will see in the following section.

Before going into this question, however, it should be remembered here that "teachers have always complained," and that they are considered badly paid throughout Latin America. The principal comment our informants gave on this point referred to the stability that government-employed teachers enjoyed previously. In addition, they mentioned the free access to health care and education they had had for their children. The biographies we have studied allow us to infer that, while the majority of teachers always began their careers with ups and downs, sooner or later each one did achieve job stability.

Both the older teachers and the younger ones (less surprisingly) have all had complex occupational histories, which have been economically precarious and sometimes unstable as well. But the instability for the older teachers was always *temporary*. Once they got themselves installed in their posts, they lived, like all members of the middle classes, with certain economic difficulties and sometimes owed money, but they had job security.

The Networks

> *I have been in six schools; I have been in one of them permanently and in the others for periods. I answered an advertisement in the newspaper for one of the jobs, but I got all the others through personal contacts.*
> —Fernando Morales

> *In my experience at least, nobody escapes the help of their parents.*
> —Marcia Vidal

The use of one's network of personal contacts is fully confirmed by the occupational histories of all our informants, their living conditions, how they deal with their everyday expenses and with emergencies. Keeping a roof over one's head, getting a job or a change of work, is always accompanied by the figure of a relative or a friend (either of the informant or of the family) who acts as the contact.

Even in the more distant past, there are instances in which the informants have lived in the house of relatives or have obtained housing through relatives or friends. Later, it was almost always family contacts or connections of other sorts that led the informants to solve the problem of a home. Alvaro Canales, for example, found one of his homes "through my mother. My mother was acquainted with a person who rented a house, so she had a word with him, and . . . " A friend later rented him a house in a military township. Irma Gómez today lives in her own apartment, but her father pays the mortgage. Sonia Salas began her married life living with her mother-in-law. Fernando Morales was lent a house in Santiago when he returned from the South with very little money.

The importance of contacts in getting work is even clearer. "I had never worked with adults, not even in night school," said Morales. "Well, I was offered a few hours of classes through a friend; that's the way it works." And Félix Briones recalled that he "went to an office to register for work and overheard a conversation. One of the people was asking for teachers, I didn't catch for which subject. They took down her name; she was a principal of a school and I had heard my mother mention that name. When I got home I told my mother what had happened, and she said she knew the woman well. They had worked together for many years. So she got in touch with her friend, who immediately gave me a job." Both Santiago Peralta and Sonia

Salas got their first teaching jobs through their mothers, who were teachers themselves. Silvia Jeria got her first job thanks to a contact made for her by her sister, also a teacher.

Access to employment also frequently involves figures such as teachers the informants received their training from in the past, fellow students, colleagues or ex-colleagues, new acquaintances in the field of education, all of whom represent an extension of the informants' social network. Such was the case for Marcia Vidal and Juana Barros, for example. The quality and extension of the contacts are without any doubt linked to the informants' social extraction and, subsequently, to the type of school they attended. In the case of Irma Gómez, for instance, the fact she had attended important convent schools in Santiago was what gave her the job in a school that, albeit in a poor area of town, was a dependency of a prestigious religious college. As we have already pointed out, this same link led to her being offered a job in the college itself later on. "Although not all the teachers there come from my social class—the so-called 'impoverished gentry'—I feel that there is an element of class security—you see it in the form of participation. There's a cultural element, I don't know how to explain it . . . you have a certain vocabulary, you can speak in a self-assured manner—many teachers do not speak with confidence—and here we are in the world of the image. You either have it or you don't."

The constant presence of these contacts reveals the existence of what we earlier described as a system of reciprocal exchange of favors (or social networks). The model presented, containing a horizontal axis (representing the contacts) and a vertical one (representing the types of favors), covers—in both senses—a wide range of possibilities. The study of our interview material, however, shows a change in the model found in Figure 2.1, a change that operates in two ways:

- On the horizontal axis the network has become very limited. In fact it is reduced to the nuclear family and friends (for certain sorts of favors). Acquaintances are mentioned only with respect to getting a job or rented accommodation.
- On the vertical axis the change—obviously—refers to the types of favors. Whereas previously favors were usually of a bureaucratic sort, today they are largely concerned with survival.

In the first case it is interesting to note that politics do not appear in the networks used—especially since we are dealing with the teaching profession. Teachers as a group have always been associated formally or informally with some political position or grouping, a product of their belonging to the public sector. First, it was the Radical Party, whose first government put strong emphasis on the need to strengthen public education. "To govern is to educate," said Don Pedro Aguirre Cerda, the first Radical president. Later governments conserved this orientation, although not explicitly. They never questioned the importance of education in general nor that of public education in particular. The Christian Democrat government under Don Eduardo Frei undertook important reforms with the intention of improving public education both quantitatively and qualitatively. Christian Democracy came to replace the Radical Party both in government and in terms of political doctrine as the hegemonic force within the teaching profession. In the same way, during the Unidad Popular government, the socialist party had great influence in public administration as a whole.

After the military coup in 1973 the political parties lost all control of public administration, which explains the absence of any mention of this component in the use of networks by our informants. A new factor appeared that might be called the "military network." The armed forces in Chile have always functioned as an enclave, for reasons we do not need to analyze here. Various studies have shown that they have their own social networks and that traditionally this has not encouraged contact with civilians.

Only two of our informants referred to use of the military network, and in both cases the contact was a very close relative: the father. In the case of Alvaro Canales, his father (a retired army man) intervened to obtain the freedom of one of his own sons, Alvaro's brother. A member of the armed forces also offered Canales a house to rent at one point, and it was again thanks to these contacts that Canales managed to start a new career away from teaching. In the other case the (putative) father was the relative of a high-ranking member of the armed forces. Carlos Peña used this contact to avoid political persecution so that he could continue with his studies. He promised not to "get involved in politics" for five years. His relative managed to get the category of "dangerous," to which Peña had been assigned, changed, and Peña could go on studying.

In other words, one source of social capital—the political parties—has disappeared, without really being replaced by another, since the respective social networks, the civilian and the military, are so separate. It used to be relatively easy to ask a political contact for a favor, or to find someone with access to the required person or agency. At the same time, military men have employed a discourse that suggests that they are not willing to grant favors, that they are "incorruptible." Finally, even with the right contacts, the fact of an authoritarian military government means that both he who asks for the favor and he who grants the favor act in fear. Reticence is also explained by the fact that an element of trust or intimacy (confianza) enters into the exchange of favors. In order to request a favor, one has to be sufficiently familiar with the person one is going to ask or who is going to introduce one to the potential source. Before asking for the favor, the degree of confianza one has with the person who is in the position to help is automatically evaluated. All this is not to say that such a network does not exist; it exists for some, as can be seen in the cases we have summarized. But since its use is far more limited, the impossibility of using political contacts appears as a net loss for the immense majority of the members of the middle class we have studied.

The second case—the change on the vertical axis of our network model—can be observed in the continual mention of favors connected with the physical survival of the informants being received (or granted). Santiago Peralta, for instance, explains how he has been able to survive. "During quite a long period of time my father-in-law used to send us and his son in the North a box of provisions—sugar, flour, oil; the most expensive things, I would say."

Juana Barros, on the other hand, plans to put her son into a school. "I will spend at least 10,000 pesos, and then he can go and have lunch with my mother. My mother will help us out once again." Sonia Salas also mentioned help with food. "On one of the occasions that I was out of work—I don't remember which one, I was giving a course of further education for teachers (I've never been thrown out of that particular type of work)—my colleagues decided to give me a present. I realized something was going on because they asked me to leave the room because they were going to discuss something that I couldn't listen to. They decided, by majority vote, to give me a food basket. I think it was a majority decision because some of them seemed very embarrassed when the food basket arrived. . . . I was very touched by the fact that everything came from their own homes. However, I did notice that some of them were very perturbed; they didn't know whether I would be offended. Some of them felt it wasn't really 'the right thing to do.' In fact, for me it was one of the most sensitive gifts I have ever received, that is, it was a projection of the feeling of solidarity."

Salas's particular personality allowed her to receive this gift without feeling shame. But the perturbation that she perceived in her colleagues undoubtedly reflects a far more generalized sentiment among the middle class when the need for material help in something as basic as food is made manifest.

Our informants also talked about the help they received in caring for their children. This help usually came from the mother of one of the couple, or from a sister or sister-in-law. The family network appeared as almost the only possible source of assistance, or, at least, the only one our particular subjects sought to use. In only one case did the informant mention a neighbor who sporadically looked after her children for her, this favor being reciprocated by the informant.

Health care, particularly in the case of children, is another type of favor required of the network. Juana Barros told us that "you have to have money to go to the doctor; if not your child can just die. So I went out and telephoned from the hospital: 'please, I need money, can you help?' Yes, they had a checkbook, no problem, and they came and stayed with me too." Santiago Peralta mentioned another example. "If I have a major emergency, I have two friends who are doctors and whom I can call and say, 'You know I haven't a cent' ... and they always treat my children free with no problem. ... They even give me the money to get home again."

Where money is concerned, most of the demands are channeled through the family, especially if there is an emergency requiring large sums. To "get to the end of the month," a colleague or a friend can be asked for help. The majority reject the idea of going to a bank because interest rates are high and they are afraid of not being able to pay back on time. According to Félix Briones, there are few possibilities of getting help in this area. "Work and the family is more or less all there is. We are a large family. But if I were to go to a bank, the interest would be enormous, a very different story."

This testimony is supported by Sonia Salas. "My mother is like an open credit line. That is, any difficulty I have, she can lend me money, and as long as I can pay her back I accept her help. She has offered me money when I have no prospect of being able to pay her back. On those occasions I don't take it—only when I know it's for two or three days, for ten days, when I know I have something coming in. But if I haven't a cent, and she offers me a loan, I won't accept it. That is, I can't accept money from anyone if I don't know when I'll be able to pay it back." Here, there is a strong element of reciprocity, one of the features of the use of the networks. The impossibility of reciprocating inhibits any request, since the situation would no longer be one of the exchange of favors between equals, which is what characterizes the use of networks in the middle class.

At any rate, the type of favors we have summarized here are very different from those described in the model of middle-class networks that emerged from the 1968 research, and closer to the type that appeared in Lomnitz's study of the marginal poor in Mexico. These two changes in the coordinates of the model reveal a serious decline in the status of teachers, a sector of the middle classes that was forcibly privatized by the predominant economic model, in the sense that it was thrown onto the labor market, with a considerable loss of prerogatives—job stability, salary increases, social security, and so on.

The teacher has been affected on two levels: the first, that of physical survival, we have just looked at. The second is related to teachers' self-esteem and their role in society within the symbolic construction of the middle class. This perception of role referring to what one is in society is a necessity. It is what confers *dignity*. In the case of teachers, apart from being badly paid and having lost their security, they have been deprived of their image of servants of an estado docente and, as a result, of their self-concept as transmitters of the history, traditions, and culture of the country. The demand most frequently mentioned in recent times by the profession—through the Colegio de Profesores—is the recovery of dignity, both of the profession and of the teacher.

When a teacher discusses his conditions of work with a mayor, he is not just negotiating his pay, but also his position in society. From the moment he is told that, if he does not agree with the conditions of work offered, he can leave, the status he has internalized over the years of belonging to a sector of the state responsible for the training of future generations is eroded. This role of the teaching profession has never been questioned, even today—at the level of discourse. But while we carried out our interviews for this study, it became very clear that teachers felt this aspect of their symbolic self-construction had been affected at least as much as the material aspects of their lives, if not more.

The Vision of Teaching

> *The mystique of our profession is a cultural question in our country. We get ex-students coming here comparing their ideals with the conditions of work, but no one leaves the profession.*
> —Ivan Navarro

Our informants confirmed the appreciation of Navarro, the director of a teacher-training institute. However, the interviews also confirmed—in most cases—the generalized impression that not all teachers choose their profession because they feel a strong vocation. Many of them do so because they started teaching, while they were still in high school, as a way of earning a living not requiring any previous studies, or else because their mother or another relative was a teacher and got them jobs in their schools, or because their marks on the Prueba de Aptitud Académica (PAA; or Academic Aptitude Test) were low and they qualified for university entrance only in pedagogy.

Nevertheless, today they all declare that they could not live without teaching. With the exception of Alvaro Canales, who could not continue because he had not graduated, the rest all continue to teach. But even Canales says: "I think that the years will go by—perhaps I'll always be saying the same thing, but maybe there is still the chance that one day I'll finish my degree and be a qualified teacher." He also told us of conversations with other ex-teachers, friends of his who had had to leave the profession, who were out of work or employed in some other activity. They are all frustrated. "One of them told me, 'What I wouldn't give to be back in the classroom!' I replied, 'But don't you realize you're probably earning more now?' And he said, 'There's always a feeling of emptiness, something pulls me back toward teaching.'" For Graciela Berríos, dismissed after the military coup of 1973, who fought to be reincorporated into teaching, the return to the classroom was a wonderful moment. "For me, to have managed to get back there, up in front of the pupils again, was marvelous. I didn't care that it was the night shift, nothing else mattered. To be teaching again really pulled me up, absolutely." Given the story of how many of the teachers became teachers in the first place, such an expression of professional vocation appears contradictory, difficult to account for. A possible explanation could be the mystique (*mística*) mentioned by Navarro. This spiritual aspect or attachment to the profession may well develop during professional studies, or else is a consequence of the experience of teaching itself, or both.

Many informants spoke of the importance of their contact with reality as a result of teaching. This aspect appears as an impetus to carry on in spite of the precarious living conditions they have to face. For instance, Félix Briones said: "Obviously, you have to be a magician. Thank God I'm involved in a part of the system, a very low-level part. And I thank God because being where I am means that I can see reality. Apart from the material poverty, there is a spiritual poverty that is the poverty of the future. . . . I work in an elementary school and in a high school at the moment, and I have pupils who haven't even got a future."

Marcia Vidal also values the contact with reality produced by the incorporation of her study group "Spaces" into the Instituto de Perfeccionamiento (Further Studies Institute) del PIIE. "We did it because we realized that we were becoming isolated, that there was no point in just the alternative schools doing things. It was a task for the whole profession. There was no sense in having a nice time in Spaces, feeling we were doing something interesting because we had conditions that permitted us to do so. I feel the institute has changed our lives, because it put us right into the profession with the ordinary teachers who live and work in the most terrible realities, so giving a course there is quite different."

Many of the informants insisted on the need for further education, and either took courses or had some sort of research activity. All the informants mentioned the function of education and told us their opinions on the subject. Félix Briones said: "The children have to be stimulated. We have to motivate them, we can't always be doing the same thing, we can't stagnate. The teacher has to revise and renew his courses, taking into account the interests of the children." Success after such efforts gives great satisfaction, said Briones, although he added that in his view not all teachers were interested enough; it depended on their values. "These are the satisfactions of being a teacher. But they can't be put into the cooking pot, as they say. I don't live off them, but, deep down, one's vanity, one's ego receives a big boost. Now, something that is very important is that, according to how you see the world, you give more importance to one or another aspect. Working in two schools enables me to compare levels of education: how the pupils in one school compare with the pupils in the other; what one teacher gives of himself and what another teacher gives: 'so much you pay me, so much I give.' I was talking about this very question recently with a colleague; in the private subsidized school things are cold and inhuman."

Ernesto Maldonado, as an educator, researcher, and counselor of many years' experience, is very critical of the training new teachers are getting, sometimes in the hands of persons trained abroad, incapable of understanding Chilean reality. "They finish very badly trained. They have instrumental knowledge for given subjects, but they don't understand the problem, the role the educator fulfils in this cultural context. They despise it and they know nothing about it. They turn their backs and don't accept it. . . . Teachers in the past also tended to do the same, but with a difference. The teachers from the old training colleges had a greater commitment and were closer . . . let's say, their social extraction was different, they were more humble, they had a greater commitment to the poor."

Various informants saw the moral value of teaching, of fulfilling the role of educator, as a counterbalance to the bad pay. The spiritual satisfactions compensate for the deficiencies resulting from material deterioration. Morales remarked: "Well, the mystique is what keeps me here. And I think that is what has saved education so far. Fortunately, there is a good level of teaching, it could be better, despite what we're paid. I think that one has always known what teachers earn . . . so I don't justify mediocrity because of the low pay. I understand it, but I don't justify it, especially since we teachers have a flexibility, a versatility—how shall I put it?—we have a minimum of the minimum that helps us a lot when it comes to trying other things. . . . But if it weren't for the fact that there is still a certain amount of mística, vocation, affection, appreciation of young people in general, things would be a lot worse. I think that is what is saving the profession at the moment. . . . The people with most ideas and questions, the ones that get most involved in teaching, are the ones that find most obstacles in the system."

According to Juana Barros, the desire to take further training courses is also frustrated by obstacles that can be overcome only by a strong vocation. "Entry to the courses (of the PIIE) is not as difficult as completing them . . . because normally this type of course is not given any value by the institution where you work. Furthermore, they require time without offering any extra money coming in; they take away time you could be spending with your family; they take away your free time, and you receive no recognition in your place of work. I think you have to have a very strong vocation."

While neither a teaching vocation nor the mystique or spiritual aspect of the profession appear a priori in most of the cases we studied earlier, today they are very marked, again in most of the informants. The exception—and it is not a clear-cut one—is Marcia Vidal, the youngest of the group (twenty-four). "Most of the people I know of my age or of my generation all reach a moment in which they rethink their career. It is like thinking about yourself from the beginning again. In your mind you ask yourself, 'Have I chosen the right career, or is it perhaps just something nice to do?' Independently of whether it is nice or not, you need a lot of patience and vocation, nerves of steel and all that. And then you start thinking about practical matters, like survival and how to support the children you want to have and how to send them to a good school and how you want to carry on studying. For other people these questions are perhaps very normal, but they're difficult for us. So then you finally ask yourself, 'Am I going to carry on with this or not? Is it worth it, all this sacrifice?' I don't know if everyone has these moments of doubt, but I certainly have and so have a lot of the people I know."

Of our informants, only one (Canales) left teaching, and not because he wanted to. Throughout his interview he repeatedly referred to his desire to return to teaching. "I have always said and I still do, the day that the circumstances are right, I am going to see if I can go back to teaching. I would like to work in education in any capacity; that is, I'd like to go back to being who I really am; it's what I'm trained for, it's what I did for many years, and it's something inside me that I can't just rub out, just like that."

Teaching could not "be rubbed out just like that" in the case of Briones either, even if a stroke of luck were to make him into a millionaire. "Here in my family we do a lot of daydreaming. For instance, we imagine we suddenly have a stroke of luck (I think everyone has fantasies of this sort sometimes). Well, even in that case, for me the idea of continuing to teach is always there, even if only part-time."

6
Teachers' Lives: Five Cases

In this chapter, in greater depth and without commentary, we present life stories that one way or another illustrate what we have written in earlier chapters and also in our conclusions. These autobiographies are those of:

- *Félix Briones, a physical education teacher, thirty-eight years old, married;*
- *Sonia Salas, a philosophy teacher, forty years old, separated;*
- *Marcia Vidal, an elementary school teacher, twenty-four years old, unmarried;*
- *Alvaro Canales, a mathematics teacher, forty-three years old, married; and*
- *Fernando Morales, a high school biology teacher, thirty-two years old, married.*

Perpetual Anxiety: Félix Briones

I come from a family of teachers, and the vast majority of them are teachers for reasons of tradition. We teach different subjects, although naturally some of us coincide. I have twin cousins who are teachers. My sister studied in the Escuela Normal and then in the university. I teach physical education. My mother is a retired elementary school teacher.

My father was a public employee in Valdivia. My sister and I went to school for a few years in Valdivia and then carried on here in Santiago. We came to Santiago when we were still quite young, seven or eight years old more or less. We studied both elementary and high school in public schools. We both entered the Escuela Normal, and my sister went on to the university before finishing. She went to the Pedagógico of the Universidad Técnica. She graduated and began to work in a high school. She had been teaching in an elementary school, but she left there when she qualified as a high school teacher and started working here in Santiago in a prestigious government-run high school. They took into account the years she had already worked while she was still studying. Before, they used to allow people who were studying in the Escuela Normal to start working straight away in some schools. My sister must have nearly twenty years of service by now, I think.

In my case, I finished high school and started to work. I was studying mechanical engineering in Temuco for almost a year, but I didn't like it, I couldn't settle down for various reasons and ended up back in Santiago. Before that I had been a year—a wasted year, too—in the Escuela de Carabineros. My father wanted me to be a policeman, but I didn't like that either. Finally I took the Prueba de Aptitud Académica again and did badly. I tried to get into the Escuela Normal as a last resort. No, no, that's not quite how it was, I was working. I started work in a government office. During 1969 and 1970 I was working and then I decided to try studying again. I took the test, did badly, and went to teacher-training college because of my low marks.

I [had] found work thanks to a friend, a school friend that I bumped into one day. During the summer vacations there was voluntary work; that is, you went off to build schools, teach people to read and write in the provinces, and there I met this friend who offered me a job and I was attracted by the chance to stay in Santiago. The following day I should have traveled south. This friend put me in touch with the people who more or less decided who got a job and who didn't. I worked there for two years. The job was in a government agency, and I got on very well; very well, not because I'm outstanding, very intelligent, or anything like that, no, but because I was young and the people working there were older and they had sort of stagnated. So I began to move up the ladder quite fast, and they sent me off to do some courses, and there I decided I ought to carry on studying and ended up entering the Escuela Normal.

[Then the coup fell on Chile.] I wasn't involved in politics . . . I had my ideals but I didn't participate actively, I wasn't committed in any particular way. So when the coup came, I stayed put. I was twenty-three, and then the year ended and the following year . . . the following year I went on studying. The Escuela Normal had been closed, let's say it had been done away with. It simply ceased to exist. All the students were assimilated by the universities. . . .

All this time I carried on working in the government agency. I worked there until 1975. In that year I was doing my last courses in the university in order to graduate, and I had lots of problems with my schedules because I worked mornings—during the day, let's say—and some of my subjects were in the morning and some in the evening. I had an internal arrangement with my immediate boss that allowed me to attend class during the day, but the head of the department had no idea of this and did not authorize it, since my studies were not of much use to my specific job. If I had been studying some other subject, perhaps he would have seen some advantage. I did not get the necessary authorization and began to miss work. I just missed work until they practically fired me. That was in 1975. But I did finish my studies. I was a month without a job and then began teaching.

With the Sweat of His Brow

I got this job by chance in a way, but probably without my mother's help I wouldn't have.... At that time the principals appointed their staff, not like now, now it's the mayor, the manager.... This principal [an old friend of Félix's mother] gave me a temporary job at first while I qualified. I still hadn't finished my studies. It was an elementary school in San Miguel. They gave me a few hours of physical education, but I had to be the form teacher of seventh grade. I had seven hours of classes, that was all. In two days I had done my seven hours. They were divided into six hours of physical education and one hour counseling my class. I earned very little—not even enough for the bus fare. It wasn't even a quarter of a full-time salary. But it suited me, it was a job and there was always the possibility, now that I had entered the service, of further teaching. And I was still single.

Later, by chance, while talking to some friends, I happened to mention that I needed work, that is, I wanted more teaching hours. A friend we all had in common had just resigned his teaching at two schools in order to go to work at the university, so they gave me the addresses of the schools so I could go and see if they would employ me. In one of them I got the job, but in the other the vacancy had already been filled. I completed a full-time schedule in an industrial school in Conchalí. I had what they call a full fiscal schedule [*jornada fiscal total*], which was thirty-six class hours. Half a day's work is ideal, I think, in terms of working hours; thirty-six hours. The corresponding salary at the time must have been the equivalent of around 35,000 or 40,000 pesos today.

While I was working there, I got some other things for the free time that I still had—the other half day. I started working in a company. I was put in charge of the sports club.... It was my training in physical activities, sports, folklore.... It was just before September 18 [Chile's national day], I remember, that I started working there, and in the folklore part I met Angélica. It was a private company, a big one.... I got the job through a colleague who, in turn, was a friend of the company's social worker [*asistente social*]. I earned about three times what I got giving classes in schools, working about a quarter of my working day. I worked there four days a week, two hours a day at the most, playing basketball, swimming, doing gym or folklore, and sometimes I took the teams to play elsewhere. Then suddenly, the company went bankrupt. I didn't get any indemnification because I was not under contract. I just gave them a receipt when they paid me, I had no contract. I was still single. Angélica got another job, and when she had been in her new secretarial post for a few months we got married.

I carried on teaching at the industrial school and later on they introduced the Carrera Docente, and teachers had to concentrate their activities in one school. At the time I worked in two, in San Miguel and in Conchalí; in such cases, all your teaching hours were concentrated in the school you had most hours in to start with. So, I was assigned exclusively to Conchalí. I did my full schedule there, that is, a complete half-day schedule. Later, thanks to my sister, I got another complete schedule of the same sort in the afternoons. There I earned a lot less than in Conchalí, because it was a private subsidized school at the time. I earned about 70 percent of what I got in the government school. I worked there for a year, and then they asked us to decide: they offered me the chance to work all day in the private school, or leave; I wasn't allowed to work there half-time. So I left because the offer wasn't very attractive: the full-day salary would have been only a little bit more than what I was already getting in Conchalí. I stayed on in Conchalí and applied for a transfer to Maipú.

The transfer went through. I had asked for the transfer because the industrial school was transferred to the Cámara de Construcción, and it looked as if there were going to be a lot of people thrown out. There wouldn't have been any indemnification there either. This is one of the things we've lost: stability. You can be sacked from one moment to the next, without any reason given. And the compensation . . . at present it's not more than five months' pay, one month for one year worked. I have been two years here in the corporation, since we were transferred from the municipality, so I would be paid only two months. . . . There's a lot of unemployment. Apart from that, the sostenedores—the owners of the private schools that subsidized education depends on—take advantage of the situation and pay the salaries that suit them. If I got thrown out tomorrow, and if I get paid 1,000 pesos an hour in a private school, they'll offer me 400 or 500 pesos for the same hour and I'll have to accept it. At the present time I'm in a municipal school, which is also subsidized; they're all the same really, exactly the same; the only difference is that the boss in one of them is a true boss and the other is the municipality. In practical terms, even if the school is municipal, it's also private; it's just a pretence that it is still publicly run.

When Angélica and I got married, we came to live in Maipú, so it suited me to work there. At the time transportation over there was difficult, not like now. It took me about an hour and a half to get to Conchalí. After we'd been married about two years I managed to get transferred over here. I had one job, earning . . . in terms of today, about 35,000 pesos, something like that. A very low income. At the time the rent we paid was about—must have been half my salary, a bit less perhaps, around 15,000 pesos. I don't remember very well, but it was a high rent for us. Of course, Angélica carried on working.

Later, while I was working in Maipú, one day I went to see my sister, who told me that she had recently met up with a friend, a neighbor, who had asked after me, whether I was working. This neighbor asked my sister to tell me to get in touch with her because she worked in a school here in Maipú that needed a teacher of physical education. I went over there straight away, and they offered me a job here in the school I'm working in now. At the time it was a parochial school. Now it's private and subsidized. So I started working in two schools, in the private academy and in the public school that later became municipal. And that's been the situation to this day. . . .

There are two systems of retirement now: some people continue in the Caja de Empleados Públicos [Public Employees Fund], the old system, and others . . . are in the AFP [Retirement Fund Administration]. The ones in the old system retire after thirty years' service and are the minority; there are very few of them, very few, because the vast majority changed over to the new system because it meant paying out less every month, so it was like your salary was larger. That is, if you were in the old system, you received 30,000 pesos net every month, while the person who had opted for the new system got 32,000. This is logical because one doesn't think of the future, one thinks of today. The new scheme means smaller monthly deductions but lengthens the years of service before retirement. Let me explain: before, you used to retire after thirty years of service; now the women retire at sixty years of age and the men at sixty-five.

Other things that we lost were the *concursos* [competitions] and the cátedras. Now we've lost the administrative statute. The concurso meant you presented your CV [curriculum vitae]; it encouraged you to go on studying, et cetera, to improve yourself professionally. Today, a person can start his first job earning exactly the same as someone who has twenty years' service. The salary goes up when there are adjustments. There's no incentive. There's talk of a minimum wage, but the fact is that there's so much unemployment that people accept whatever they're offered. I get 42,000 pesos net in the municipal school for thirty hours. In the other school I get 41,000 pesos for twenty-five hours. I work from eight o'clock in the morning to seven o'clock at night every day, including Saturdays. Whatever was better in the past is worse today. In my case, the publicly run schools paid much better than the private ones in the past. Today, it's the other way round, because I get 42,000 pesos for thirty hours in the former and 41,000 for twenty-five hours in the latter; thus I get paid more in the private school.

Now there are people who were mistakenly classified when the transfer occurred. Let me explain; some of them should have been in A, for example, but were put into B, and to this day their situation has not been sorted out. I have colleagues who had not graduated when the transfer occurred—well, their degree was in process of being issued, but they figured on the register as not having graduated—but who later received their degree certificate. When they got their certificate it was recognized on paper, but not in their pay. They're still paid as if they hadn't graduated, when they should have been reclassified and moved up to grade eighteen at least, once they had their degrees. During the last fifteen years, no one has been given a raise or been reclassified, we're all stuck where we were before. What's the point of studying? There's no incentive. People have stopped doing it. Furthermore, you've got to pay for further education, so why bother if it will never be reflected in your salary? Nowadays I think that if anyone wants to study pedagogy, they've got to be very aware of what they can hope to earn. Perhaps even more to the point is that few people can afford to study. . . . It's very difficult because many jobs require qualifications.

The Domestic Economy

I earn 83,000 pesos, and my wife earns about the same. We each pay 50 percent of the [fixed] household expenses. We pay a mortgage on the house [in unidades de fomento]* of about 15,000 pesos. . . . Our son attends the school I work in, and it's free. But our daughter attends a private school, and we pay around 13,000 pesos, including transport. We decided to send her there because it's a good school, run by a religious order. She is just starting, and we thought it was for the best, part of the sacrifice we have to make. But the car—if there's enough money we use it, if not we don't. . . . Angélica usually takes care of our daughter, and I cover our son's needs for clothing, et cetera. As far as our clothing is concerned, if there's money we buy some, and if not we don't, but it doesn't worry us. The children are our first priority, and the house too. We do have a maid. We pay her 12,000 pesos at the moment, but at the end of this month her wages will go up because that was the agreement. We have been long periods without anyone to help look after the children. . . . This maid we have now was sent from heaven when my ulcer (I have a duodenal ulcer) was about to give out.

At the moment I am on sick leave from both my schools. This is also a problem. I don't know what it's like in other places, but here it's as follows: when you're on sick leave you don't get all your salary; that is, you lose 30 percent. If you add on all the rest of the extra money you spend when you're sick (doctors, medicines), it comes out to quite a lot. And then if you have to register at the hospital . . . Our case is as follows, every month they take off a percentage of your salary, which goes into a health fund [*fondo de salud*]. You can choose where the fund is deposited, with a government agency or with a private organization (the Isapre). They administer the fund, and when you need a doctor or medical attention of some sort, they tell you how much you have to pay for whichever service you need, but you have to pay. If you can't pay, you don't get any medical care. Other types of hospitals . . . hardly any. You have to go and get an appointment; you have to get up early in the morning to get an appointment with a doctor; then if you need hospital attention, you have to wait for months on end. When finally you get to be admitted to the hospital, you have to take your own medicine, there aren't any sheets on the beds, there is a lack of many of the basics. Now, when you realize that the attention in these hospitals is bad, logically you have

---

*Editors' note: Unidades de fomento is a parallel monetary system that changes daily according to the inflationary index, plus the value of the dollar in the country. A mortgage is not contracted in pesos, but in unidades de fomento, which go up constantly in pesos.

to go where the attention is at least half decent and there you have to pay.

We have our expenses very well organized. This means we manage, for example, to eat meat nearly every day. That is also why our life is more or less okay, much better than many other people's, but for us, it is only satisfactory, because we don't really have a feeling of true comfort and well-being. I understand that to include rest and recreation. One should work, and then when the vacations come, one should have a chance to get away somewhere—this isn't really our case. Usually in the vacations we go south, camping. I ask for a loan for these trips—from a company that is linked with the school. Using the money for a vacation is allowed. Otherwise we could go away only if we saved up, and we don't do that.

So how do we survive? As long as we are orderly, and we are very orderly—Angélica is more organized than I am—we work out our monthly expenses and we plan for the whole year. We spend according to what we earn. There are variations of course. Food expenses vary a lot; food tends to go up in price. For example, in September we have 34,000 pesos for the supermarket. Vegetables and bread have to be added to that. In this household the only item that gets bought on a daily basis is bread; the rest is bought once a month, and fruit and vegetables on the weekends. They cost about 12,000 pesos a month. For bigger items, we buy something once I've finished paying for the previous purchase. There's a system here whereby you can buy something and pay for it in three installments without paying interest. We have bought some things using this system. That is the way we manage. . . .

There's always something comes up that you haven't budgeted for. The children are growing up, they grow out of their shoes and their clothing. We have fixed expenses like electricity, gas, supermarket, the woman that helps with the children, the mortgage. These are all fixed expenses. Recreation, for example, isn't included in our budget. But we do get a bonus at the national holiday and at Christmas. This year they gave us the equivalent of 20 percent of our salary in the municipal school and the same in the other school. We got, together [i.e., from Félix's two schools], about 15,000 pesos, not counting what Angélica receives. This means that this month it will be easier to make ends meet. I've been calculating our expenses for this month, mainly what we'll have to spend at the supermarket, which is where the prices change most. I noted down all the things we buy in the supermarket, and this month we just won't be able to manage. Everything has gone up a lot. Between the month before last, August, and September, we had a difference of just over 7,000 pesos, from 26,500 to 33,800. And this has to be paid somehow or other. This happens nearly every month. Once, the difference was in our favor, minimally, not even 1,000 pesos, from 27,300 to 26,500. But the next month it was 29,000 pesos, so it's always the same. This is what makes it easy not even to notice when there is someone to help with the children, because the money would just go on something else that wasn't in the budget, although one ought to try to save. Ice cream, for example, we don't put that in the budget; a soft drink now and then, an outing . . . but we never go to the movies, it's ten years since we went to the movies. We have been to the theater. Then we ask the lady that helps with the children to stay overnight, sometimes my mother-in-law comes—somehow we manage.

Now, our social life, more than a social life, consists of relaxing by doing what the children enjoy doing; we accompany them on their outings. They belong to a scout troop, so when they go camping, we go with them. We get enjoyment out of what they like. If they play sports, we go along too. We go to mass, to buy plants, and while all these things cost money they are also recreational. . . . We can do this more easily because as the children grow up there are more things they can do. For example, usually during my two-month summer holiday, I take a job in January. Before I worked January and February, but now I work only January, giving swimming classes in a municipal pool in the neighborhood. This also gives us a little extra money to spend when we go out.

SOS

We have a lot of contact with my wife's family. This is very normal; it's normal, let's say, in the case of the man. In general, married men have more contact with their wife's families than vice versa. Perhaps it's caused by maternal selfishness; jealousy on the part of the mothers of men toward their daughters-in-law leads to greater, more fluid contact with the man's mother-in-law. The relationship always seems much better. In our case the relationship is extremely good. Thus, I have a rather distant relationship with my own sister. That too appears to be pretty common.

Now, should I have an emergency involving money, I go to my place of work; to one of them, the private school. We have an internal relief system that charges a minimal interest rate. Mind you, if you've already got one loan, they don't lend you any more. In that case you go straight to the school principal, and he lends you money out of his own pocket, without interest, without expecting anything in return. We are privileged in this sense. We can resort to the school if Angélica's family or one of my own relatives can't help out. Apart from the alternative of the school, we have the in-laws. It's a mutual thing. We used to ask my mother-in-law when we needed something for the children. My mother-in-law practically brought my son up. They also came to live here, and live just around the corner. But she's getting on now and can't help us with the children. They live with another married son, and my sister-in-law also works so they can't help us with our little girl. She also has a woman who helps her with the children.

Going back to money emergencies: when faced with unexpected, unforeseen events—illness, a broken-down refrigerator—what do we do? Well, I have to pay a given number of things every month; maybe I just don't pay one of them. What can one play with in this way? Electricity is one. If I don't pay this month, I just get a bill next month for two months. If this month's bill is 2,000 pesos, next month's bill will come for 4,000, but I can go and ask for the 4,000 to be divided into installments, with interest. And this will finally allow me to deal with the unexpected event, and I just have to pay a little bit more for the electricity. I try to handle things without bothering anybody. . . . In the school, there's a low interest to keep the fund going, but it is minimal. But we don't have to use the school fund too often, since we both work, which is a great help. This isn't so in every family. I couldn't maintain the family by myself.

Friends and Colleagues: The Labor Union

My children are my best friends. I have few friends, and I maintain some friendships from childhood with people who, for one reason or another, one stops seeing for a time and then suddenly they reappear in one's life. Through Angélica I have met up with some people again. I have two childhood friends whom I have met up with again after many years, although we never forgot each other. They work in a company that has to do with journalism. One of them is a journalist. I have a friend in the private school; the rest are colleagues with whom the relationship is more one of respect. I've got other friends that aren't connected with teaching, friends I share with Angélica. . . . With my brothers-in-law there is more than the family connection, there's also friendship, affinity. . . . I have tried not to center my life only on my work. I come from a family of teachers, and the conversations are always about the same thing—teaching—so I try to avoid it because you have to take a rest from work sometimes.

The teachers' organizations here in this neighborhood—I feel that here it's like another country, like another Santiago, another Chile; for me personally going to Santiago means something like getting ready to go to Santiago, even though its only about half an hour away. But I haven't been there for a long time; usually months go by, so I always find something new there, some new building but that's all. . . . With the teachers' organizations I feel it's exactly the same. We're so far away from the top. We have sort of grown apart. The national leader throws a stone and then hides his hand; in contrast, the rank-and-file member throws the stone and stands up to be counted, whatever might happen. My view is that you have to be objective and realistic; I can't dream of utopias and hope to fix my life that way. I'll tell you what Angélica and I were talking about the other day. I had heard that there had been another list of demands presented by the Colegio de Profesores on the occasion of Teachers' Day. They were talking about the salaries they were demanding. Of course, ideally, my God, I wish we could get them! But if you are earning a salary of 30,000 or 40,000 pesos, which is of course very little, its absurd to ask for a raise taking the salary up to 120,000 pesos, even though it should be more. But let's be realistic. If they pay what they do with difficulty, it's ridiculous to think they can pay three times as much. It's laughable. It's preferable to ask for what you're likely to get—it's like a utopia, it's like saying I'm going to buy this lottery ticket because I'm going to win.

I think that the teachers' leaders don't really respond to our expectations. Here in Maipú, for example, I worked quite a lot in the last elections . . . a lot, I was very active. Now, participating is not well looked upon, people hide the fact that they belong to the organization, or that they go to meetings. . . . I think it is a challenge to the workers, it is a challenge for the teachers to get organized. But in terms of the union itself, the Colegio de Profesores, as far as I can see, there's never any work done except in the campaign, and none afterward when the elections have been won. Of course, there are local demands made, but they have no power. For example, if a teacher is fired, they act, but their action doesn't go beyond giving him legal advice so he can try to get a compensation, not to get him reinstated. I feel it's a professional association that asks only for things that are never granted. And serves to maintain some sort of identity, of course. That is today; tomorrow, let's hope that it will function better. At the moment, at a municipal level, the association can't do anything at all.

Now, the *internal* union within the school has more power because it belongs there, it is part of the school. But though they are legal, not all schools have them, as there is a risk of being fired. That is why, usually, in the unions—look, here in the municipal corporation there is a union, but only the members of the leadership are known, and not even to all members. Only they know about it. Of course, because they have fired union leaders too. They have been fired, transferred. So, what happens? The municipal corporation has maybe twenty-five schools and in one of them there is a union. But the boss is the same, so each school is a bit like a section of the corporation. So they transfer the union people to a school where there's no union. That's what happened in this school, they transferred the whole lot, but the teachers sued the corporation and won. So the corporation, apart from losing the case, lost out economically because it had to pay the legal costs. . . . So now it just leaves the union people alone, because it can mean losing money as well as prestige.

A Teacher's Point of View

I work a half day but it's almost as if I worked all day. There's always something to be done in the afternoon, some sports activity. Of course, I don't have to correct exam papers like other colleagues, but I prepare my classes just as they do. . . . This year I have been working with small children in the private school. This has been a very useful experience for me. There are three of us teaching physical education in the school. They give us the schedule and let us divide it up among ourselves. So we have a certain amount of choice regarding which particular courses we give. In the other school it's different. There they just tell you what classes you have to teach. Well, this year I opted to teach up to sixth grade of elementary school only. First, to suit my own schedule and in part to try something new, and I've found it an incredibly enriching experience. I've felt I am giving more to my work as a result of a change within myself because I found myself teaching my own son; I know what interests him and so I could generalize a bit to the others and plan my classes on that basis, without ignoring the school's program of course. The children seem to have responded well. Now that I'm on leave, when I go out (I don't have to stay in bed) I sometimes meet some of the children from the school, in the market or somewhere else, and they ask me when I'll be back at school. "When are you coming back?" they ask me, concerned not so much about my health as about when they can have their classes with me again. Even though there is a person substituting for me at the moment, the children are not happy with him.

[Félix reflects on how teachers affect each other.] Spiritual solidarity (moral support) is so important, sometimes more important than economic support. In the private school there is real concern. A little while ago, two weeks ago it was, Teachers' Day was celebrated. The school principal made a point of inviting me to come and share in the meal with everyone. He knew I was on a special diet and was prepared to have something special cooked for me. These small details, which have nothing to do with money, are so very important. In contrast, the other school is very cold. I've always tried to foster a cordial atmosphere. The other day I was talking to a colleague about the things that affected me a lot, and, after analyzing them, I came to the conclusion that there are some things there's no point trying to change. I decided that we could do with some of what we were taught, what used to be called good manners. Yesterday I had to go and get my salary at the other school, and the principal gave it to me as if we had been seeing each other every day. I am on sick leave, and she didn't think of asking me how I felt, not even to find out if I was going to be able to return to work or not. These things are important.

What a difference in realities there is! . . . I want to talk about this, this difference in realities. Of course, there is education according to category. There are different levels; the higher the subsidy per pupil, the better the education. . . . [The sostenedor] logically prefers the child [over the teacher]. This is why one has to be aware, one has to really like the profession. My opinion is that you aren't born with a vocation. What I have seen in my life is that vocation is acquired, and more than that, what the job really is, is a necessity. This is one of the subjects I've discussed with my family a lot. There is a word that is fundamental in life for me—the word *transcendental*. One's children are transcendental; they changed my life, and from that point of view anyone can give classes. Thus, I say that from that point of view vocation is acquired with time, it's not something you're born with.

[Briones reflects with anguish on the lives his pupils face—"not a future that you can call promising or full of hope."] I won't say anything about their parents . . . of course, the economic level is very, very low and the kids are the product of drug addiction and alcoholism. . . . I have one group in the high school, and those kids are not going anywhere, although at least they haven't abandoned school. Potentially, they have nothing, nature gave them nothing, because they are the product of their parents, alcoholics, drug addicts, so . . . what can you ask of these kids? If they finish sixth grade of elementary school, they've done well. One can only practice a sort of paternalism with these kids. You can't throw them out because it affects the school's income. What's more, if they don't come to school, someone is sent off to look for them so the school doesn't lose the subsidy.

A Perpetual Quest: Sonia Salas

I am a philosophy teacher. I have also a post—coordinator, researcher in the field of group learning processes; while neither of these have helped me much as far as survival is concerned, there is a sense in which they have helped a bit.

My father finished high school and worked in a bank, first in the provinces and later in Santiago. Soon after moving to the capital, he retired because of illness. He died of cancer when he was forty-three.

My mother, Bernarda, was a primary school teacher. She wasn't able to get a proper education. She began to teach without studying. She didn't go to teacher-training college, but she did manage to qualify much later on, when she was middle-aged. You used to be able to do that. Her qualification was authorized on the basis of the number of years she had worked as a teacher. Furthermore she came from a family of trained primary school teachers. As far as I can remember, the first must have been my Uncle Fernando. He's now eighty years old, eighty-one perhaps. He's my mother's brother. He's the first teacher I remember in the family; there might have been others in earlier generations, but I can't recall. My mother's brothers and sisters were Uncle Fernando, Aunt Marisol, Aunt María, Uncle Reinaldo, Aunt Paulina. Three of them were teachers, and mother too. That is, four teachers, three from the teacher-training college, and my mother, self-taught, because there wasn't enough money for her to go to college. . . .

My grandparents . . . I don't know much about them except that my mother's father was some sort of farmer, but it appears he knew how to enjoy himself, gambling and things like that, and lost everything and then died, leaving my grandmother a young widow. Somehow or other they survived, I don't know how because I never heard anything about my grandmother's earning any money. What I do know is that they mostly lived together with relatives and close friends, or rented tiny apartments. As far as studies were concerned, it was my Uncle Fernando who made sure that everyone went to school and studied. That was his way of helping.

More Teachers

Many of my aunts' and uncles' children became teachers. My Uncle Fernando had two children who are both teachers: my cousin Aurora, who's the same age as I am, didn't study teaching, she just started teaching and later got her qualification; my cousin Francisco graduated from teacher-training college but then worked as a teacher for only a year; he works in something else now. Uncle Reinald—no, none of his children became teachers. My Aunt María has two children who are teachers: my cousin Renato, who is now dean in some Central American university; and my cousin Daisy, who teaches French and is a student counselor. It's odd that except for Uncle Fernando, whose two children are elementary school teachers (but both with a higher economic status than their parents because my cousin Aurora works in a private school where she gets very well paid, and my cousin Fernando left the profession because it didn't pay enough and now has his own firm and a different economic level), the rest, my Aunt María's children, teach high school, not elementary school like their parents. And Uncle Reinaldo's children that aren't teachers also have a higher status: one of them is a physiotherapist and the other is a civil engineer. Then there's me.

My mother didn't let me go to teacher-training college. I wanted to study to be an elementary school teacher, but she was against it. Even today, I feel it's what I like most, that is, I'm more attracted to elementary education than to high school. I think it's because when the children get to high school they have already developed bad habits of study. I like the small children very much.

One of my brothers teaches in elementary school, although he trained to teach in high school, but in his case it was pure chance, or maybe he had it "in his blood," as they say. We are from a family of teachers, and this pulls us toward the profession. He studied to be a high school art teacher but was expelled from university for political reasons. He then got his elementary school qualification thanks to the fact he was working in an elementary school. My other brother, Sandro, started to study to be an elementary school teacher but did only one year. And me, well, I'm a teacher, what else—it's the story of our family. When I chose teaching, I'm sure that all this influenced me. . . . You see, from when I was a child I observed my mother at work, and the school came to feel like my natural environment. I don't think it's just a question of whether the parent has been a good member of his or her profession or has talked a lot to the children about his or her work; no, the school just becomes your environment, your habitat.

The Beginnings

My mother began working as an elementary school teacher in the South, against my father's wishes I believe. But because of my father's illness, they came to live in the metropolitan area. However, during the early years she went to work in country towns near Santiago. We lived for ten years in the last of these, and so I spent my childhood there. It was on the road to the coast. When my father died, that is, when I was thirteen, my mother decided to return to Santiago—I don't know why. She continued to teach, that is, she applied for a transfer. She taught in an elementary school in Santiago, and we lived on her widow's pension and her salary. We didn't have our own house. We lived in all sorts of places. First of all we rented a house, a bungalow in a place called Macul. Yes, we lived in lots of different places. Then, because we had serious economic difficulties, my mother took us off to live with her brother, who was the principal of a school. We lived in the schoolhouse as sort of "guests" of the principal. My uncle was separated from his wife and had an enormous house. Besides, the situation suited him because his basic needs were satisfied, he had help with the housekeeping and other things. . . .

In fact during those years—the 1960s—we had some very difficult periods, but, all in all, things weren't so bad. My mother found a second job, employed by a municipality, giving classes in centers for mothers and in the municipality's library, so she got another salary for that.

I started studying in the university, in the Escuela de Artes Aplicadas, when my elder brother and sister still lived with us. My sister worked in a ministry. She could not continue her studies, despite the fact that she was quite a good student, because she had to help maintain the family. My brother was also working, as a salesman, without having finished high school. He could have had a successful career, given his talent, but he got married when he was twenty-one, so there wasn't much he could do to help us, nothing at all really after he was married. But my sister did help. When I was nineteen, she was killed in an accident; she was run over. Then we were left with very few resources. I think that was when we went to live with my uncle—a year later, I'm not sure. About three months later I started studying philosophy. And the family, that is, cousins, uncles, and other relatives, found me a job that would allow me to help support the family.

I was supposed to take charge of a record department in a sort of department store that I think was called Ville de Nice. I really didn't want to, I wanted to carry on studying and I resisted the pressures heroically. I went to talk to the social worker at the Pedagógico and told her my plight. She got me a study loan. First of all I never paid for tuition, never. That was 1964. I think I got the grant at the end of 1964. It wasn't a grant, it was a study loan. Besides, I had learned to make things to sell—necklaces, floral arrangements; I sold books too sometimes—so that I didn't cost the family anything. I was even able to help them. There were good and bad times, but I hardly cost the family anything.

I looked for a steady job that would be compatible with my studies and found that the fact that I was studying, instead of helping me find work, had the opposite effect, so I just sold books and things like that.

During 1966 I fell in love with a fellow student, who was a teaching assistant in the university. After dating him for a year I found I was expecting my first child; that was the reason we got married about two months later. I was already working as an elementary school teacher. It was quite common, until 1972 at least, for high school graduates to be elementary school teachers. I suppose my mother must have helped me by putting me in touch with an acquaintance of hers, but I don't remember. One of the problems for my family when I decided to get married was that I would no longer be contributing my salary to the family upkeep. I hadn't planned to have a child and had been in no hurry to get married. But the importance of my earnings for the family was such that I had to tell them everything. When I say "family" I mean my mother, my brothers and sister, my close relatives, all of whom felt, I suppose, that they were going to have to help my mother more. Uncles and brothers . . . of course, everyone got alarmed. So I explained why I had to get married; I was expecting a baby and I wanted to get married; it wasn't just because of a sense of duty to the child, I wanted to get married. But I wasn't betraying the family. At any rate, I lost the teaching job because it was only a temporary one that depended mainly on the principal. There I had my first disappointment where, let's say, "administrative measures" are concerned. The principal was a little difficult, and I had a sort of problem with her, not to do with work, although what she accused me of was always arriving late when in fact we had an agreement about that, because my classes at the university made me arrive fifteen minutes late. She had authorized this. I was finally pressured into resigning.

Going back a bit, as a child I attended that semirural school where my mother worked. It was quite a good public school. My parents supported the idea of the estado docente, and so it would never have crossed their minds to send me to a private school. I didn't think much of the private schools in our little town, which were run by nuns, and I didn't like that sort of education. I come from a family of atheists, of Communists. It was quite interesting because both my parents were Communists in their youth, but it seems my mother began to feel very unprotected after my father became ill, and my father was a very rebellious type, very unsuited to being a member of the Communist Party. He had all the features of a leader—intelligent, rebellious, difficult to get on with, didn't like following orders, for instance—he had problems at work and problems in the party; in other words, he was a bit of a disaster.

I don't think either of them were active Communists when we lived in that town. They joined the Radical Party, probably because of my father's difficulties with the Communists, but I also think that my mother wanted some kind of protection. Of course, most of the teaching profession was in line with the Radical Party, and the party itself was different then. After my father died, however, my mother returned to the Communist Party. I don't know if she ever did get any protection from the Radical Party. I suppose that she felt that it helped her get on with people better in the town, that it might give her better job security. Anyway we were the odd ones out in that town because we were practically the only atheists; my sick father was quite a character, he looked ancient when he died though he was only forty-three. People used to think he was my mother's father.

I did part of my high school education there, in a coed school. Later—it was one of the traumas of my education that stayed with me—my father took us all out of the school because he had a row with the principal's husband, who was homosexual. We had to go to school in another town, traveling in very slow buses. We had to have lunch at 11:00 A.M. in order to be there by 1:00 P.M. We were usually late. There was a lower level in the new school that left us very unmotivated. We all ended up failing the year and having to repeat. That year my father died. At first, I went back to the previous high school and then we moved to Santiago. I don't know why my mother decided to move to Santiago.

My older brother and sister had great difficulty adapting, especially my sister. I didn't. I felt very free, I felt that at last I had got away from all the prejudices of the small town; despite the fact I was only fifteen, I was already aware of them. I felt the town had been very restrictive, so the change was a good one for me, although I did have some physical problems in adapting. In Santiago, my sister started working and my brother left high school before finishing, not so much because he had to work but because he couldn't adapt.

Some of my mother's brothers and sisters lived in Santiago, like my Uncle Reinaldo, an elementary teacher. My Aunt María lived in San Bernardo, a suburb of Santiago. My mother rented a house, but the owner refused to let us have it at the last minute, I don't know why. The result was that we left an enormous house in the small town to move into a tiny apartment in Santiago, with only two rooms; it was all we could find at short notice. One room was a bedroom only, and the other was used for eating and also had two beds in it. I think this was what most affected me, because the atmosphere was dreadful. I was at a difficult age and I got the most terrible headaches, I remember. The family went to San Bernardo every Sunday, but I stayed at home just to be alone in the apartment—I didn't do anything, I just wanted to be on my own. There's a sort of pattern of illness in the family—I discovered this some years ago—it's a form of rebellion. My father's illness was in some ways a solution to his problems at work and other problems that he had adapting to reality; and since, we seem to have repeated the pattern many times—illness as a solution; it's a hypothesis. . . .

I finished high school in Santiago. I had difficulty in finding a place in a school and had to go to night school where two of my female cousins from my father's side of the family went. I settled down well there but stayed only for a few months, as my mother got the idea I was too young to be getting home after eleven o'clock at night. Santiago was dangerous, she said, and so she took me out and put me in a high school near where we lived in that two-room apartment. It was a public school for girls, quite close to home, but I never settled down there. I found it awful after being in a coed school and then in a night school—it was a school for "young ladies" . . . absurd; the teachers were rigid, old-fashioned, and elderly. Many of them corresponded perfectly to the negative stereotype of "old," that is, they were very traditional and authoritarian. I couldn't adapt and decided to leave without consulting anyone, hoping that I could take the exams anyway—the *exámenes libres*. But I couldn't because I didn't leave at the right time, according to the ministerial rules; I don't know what the problem was.

Then we moved to Macul. I remember living in at least three houses in Macul with my mother, always with problems about paying the rent and everything else. We had many economic problems at that time; sometimes we were even short of food. Our income was low, and the rest of the family could not help. On the contrary; all the cousins that studied in the Pedagógico came to us for lunch and nobody even sent over a loaf of bread. We lived near the Pedagógico. It's in that sense that I said "on the contrary."

So I finished my high school in another school for girls, again with great adaptation problems. This school did at least have a better level, but I still could not adapt. It was then that I started getting involved in politics, although the teachers didn't like it at all. The other girls who tended toward the same ideology as I did usually kept quiet about it. I left high school in 1962. I was able to finish only because I told myself I had to get out of that hell. My marks were neither good nor bad. I got good marks when I felt like it and got the minimum to pass when I didn't care. However, I did take the *Bachillerato* exams, which meant I could enter university, and came out quite well, not extraordinarily well, but well enough.

University

I didn't really know what I wanted to do with my life—I liked art a lot and was involved with folklore groups in my political party; I liked drawing and I had some talent. I liked singing and so I ended up studying in the Escuela de Artes Aplicadas. I was there for a year, but I felt I needed something more theoretical. I realized that art was very important in my life but that I needed something more speculative. I took the Bachillerato exams again; it was the only way, but I didn't manage to get high enough marks to get into psychology as I had hoped. So I went into philosophy, which I felt was the closest to what I had wanted, and assumed that I would eventually be able to transfer to psychology. The truth is I found that I liked philosophy very much. There was an atmosphere of great intellectual freedom in the department, which was at one of the best moments in its whole history. I did make some inroads into psychology, but I don't think I ever made the necessary effort to change over.

At the same time, I had my political activities, my sister died, my mother was in a very bad way, always ill—she had one problem, then depressions—so I had my hands very full. I also belonged to a folklore group; I had to start earning some money, somehow or another; I had arguments with my mother; I even left home for a year. I went to live with a friend and then started to sell books and do other things too. Once I set up a stand in a market when I was still in Artes Aplicadas, but what I sold had nothing to do with what I had learned; rather, they were things I had invented myself . . . necklaces made of seeds, floral arrangements . . . I sold quite a lot—together with the book selling, I did quite well. I had a lot of nerve; I went into offices, ministries, with my books and sold them there. At that time people read a lot, books were cheap, so I sold quite a lot . . . that way I helped with the housekeeping. . . .

Well, I was talking about when I left home. What happened finally was I had a shock because my brother, who at twenty-one had married a woman older than he, about thirty years old—well that's not so old but quite a bit older than he was—anyway, they must have had some sort of problem because they came to live with us. I was pleased to have them at first, but they fought with each other such a lot that the atmosphere at home began to be unbearable. So I left. I was a year living with a girlfriend. She lived with her grandmother, but I supported myself, that is, I paid for my own food. I didn't live off them, my friend just let me have a room. I started selling the books and then later got a job as an elementary teacher, the one that ended badly thanks to the principal. When I told my family that I was going to get married, I didn't mention the fact that I was expecting a baby. I felt my mother resented that I wasn't going to help her with money—that's what I imagined. I thought they felt that I was betraying her. We were living with my uncle by that time, as we just couldn't manage to pay a rent. That's when I got married.

Living

At first, I went to live with my mother-in-law, in a downtown apartment. My mother-in-law is quite a character; she has her funny little ways. She was furious that her only son had got married. She was a widow with an only child. Julio's father died when he was two. My mother-in-law was a real estate agent; she still is. Her husband had been a brilliant lawyer. I endured living with her for about two months. Without fighting about it, I persuaded my husband that we should have our own place. So we rented a couple of wooden rooms in a first-floor apartment near Brasil Street.

My husband was an assistant at the university and got a lot of support at that time. He is a very brilliant man. He was doing two or three assistantships, and then one of the deans gave him a temporary job in his area—yes, he got a lot of support. . . . People seemed to like us as a married couple—we were attractive, young, and intelligent . . . let's say we had a lot going for us. People wanted to help us, and since Julio worked very well, the help was warranted. He did all sorts of incredible things; he was an assistant in philosophy, biology, logic, introduction to philosophy; he taught history of art—he was like some sort of all-purpose treatment as far as university education was concerned. Meanwhile, I read, took notes, looked at slides, and we had quite a good marriage, a good relationship; we were very much in love, but I hadn't the faintest idea of how to avoid having more children. I was very ignorant in that respect and also had inherited the attitude that children just came. So I had one child after another.

I had three children with Julio, but one of them died. The first two were premature. . . . But I always managed to conserve my student status somehow or other. . . . I did three regular years, 1964, 1965, and 1966, and then my attendance got totally irregular. After I got pregnant with my first child, I kept up one subject so as to have the right to health care from the university, and the child was born at the university clinic. My first child, a boy, was born at seven months weighing only one kilo, nine hundred grams. This made me very tense and anxious. We had economic difficulties and were living in a little adobe house in a poor area of town, with no comforts. For instance, the bathroom was practically out of doors, contributing to kidney problems, cystitis, et cetera. I wasn't having an easy time of it. So, despite the fact it was a good marriage, gradually the weight of so many problems, so many children, got too much. . . . The second child was also premature and died at three months old in the hospital because we couldn't afford to pay for an incubator in a private clinic at the hospital; they just decided that he was alright and put him into the ward . . . and not only that, the doctor said that he was better off in the hospital because there he was better taken care of, that there was no point in wasting money. He was interned because of jaundice and ended up with a staphylococcus infection he picked up in the hospital.

Then we moved to an apartment out by Macul, a long way out in those days, about ten blocks from Macul, which was still more or less countryside then. My first child had asthmatic bronchitis and had a lot of choking attacks, so I had to run those ten blocks and take a taxi to the doctor. It was a complicated business and I felt, as I used to say at the time, very unfeminine; I had no milk, the baby was premature, it was like a real catastrophe, I used to say. I imagined I should be something like a woman with large breasts with lots of milk, very serene, and I wasn't anything like that; I was an intellectual, scared stiff by such tiny children . . . and my son died. I had great difficulty accepting his death. It was my mother who told me that he had died, and, for the first and last time in my life up till now, I responded by denying the death. "You're a liar," I told her. "I don't believe you." It was the day before we were to bring him home with us.

No sooner had my son died than my elder brother became ill. He had cancer, and it was discovered too late to do anything about it. He died within two months. I left my home, everything, and went to look after him. Apparently I reacted well and nursed him day and night. I had a maid; my mother-in-law helped, that is, she gave us a monthly allowance. After having tended to just lecture us on what we ought to do, she started to help. In actual fact it wasn't help, it was our right. The money came from a house that had belonged to Julio's father. That was what she gave us, so we had a maid and lived in a big house near the Plaza Italia where we rented out rooms in order to survive. We lived in two rooms and rented out the rest, so we got by.

I said earlier that when my brother died I was apparently all right. However, afterward I slept for a month, I slept and slept until one day I said to myself, "You're anemic," and I went to a doctor in the university—I don't know if it was through my husband's work there or not, I don't remember—and the doctor said that I wasn't anemic and asked me if I had had any problems. I told him that my son had died and then my brother too, and so he sent me to a psychiatrist. So I saw one whose function was to make sure I really needed help. He gave me a lot of pills, and I spent the whole weekend crying. Then I started going regularly to another psychiatrist. This one told me that it was a good thing that the medicine had made me cry, because I hadn't cried before. They had me on drugs for another month, and I was always half asleep, until one day I got fed up and went out to look for a job.

I found work in a bookshop near the Pedagógico. I really enjoyed it there. I could use my knowledge of applied art, pursue some of my own interests; I selected beautiful mural newspapers, I got to know everybody in the Pedagógico so that they didn't steal as many books as before. They were very happy to have me there, but to me it was just a game, I just wanted to overcome my depression. So, one Christmas, with masses of work and my boss in a bad mood, I resigned. I say it was a game because I really didn't need the money. I did have to help my mother, but I could do that cutting back a bit at home and could still buy my younger brothers and sisters some clothes now and again. You have to be clever managing the little you have, and I was.

Then I got pregnant with my third child, the one that is now nineteen years old. I was very happy and I wanted to have a healthy child, I wanted the child to be born at term, at nine months, so I went to the best doctors. No more university hospitals—I went to a doctor who had been strongly recommended to me. I had my daughter in a private clinic, but it was a very difficult pregnancy and I nearly lost her several times. When I was five months' pregnant, I almost lost her, but fortunately the doctor had showed me how to dose myself—increase it or reduce the dose until I could retain the baby. Now I wonder how much of my difficulty with childbearing was physical and how much was tension. Well, my daughter was born after nine months, a healthy child; three kilos and a bit she weighed. I was very happy. She was born in the springtime, so the weather was fine and I didn't have to wash thirty-odd diapers like with the other one. He had to be packed in diapers, real old-fashioned stuff; he was born in winter. And the other one had been born in the fall. So I had had a hard time with them. This time it was quite different, marvelous. She hardly needed diapers; I carried her about half-naked and she was fine.

My husband continued working. I breast-fed the baby and devoted my time to that, although I never completely lost contact. My husband edited a magazine, I collaborated; I took the odd course now and then, a seminar; I carried on studying, but not officially. I helped Julio a lot. We had what you'd call a good marriage, we were an example for most of my family, our friends, acquaintances; everyone thought of us as an excellent couple.

But I guess everything starts in the past, buried deep down—I had problems that I had not overcome. I think I was very childish in some areas of life, especially regarding sex. Then, I felt I had to get out of the house, back into life. I was in the house with the children all the time, helping my husband make progress in his work, intellectually, but I too was someone with ideas, who needed political and social activity . . . and it so happened that at the time—this was the Allende period—my mother was in charge of creating new schools. She had to go out to the slum areas and see what was needed and then decide where and when the new school would be opened. . . . There was one slum area in particular that she admired . . . she said she had never met such organized people; the leaders had such dignity, such pride.

I began to get very enthused with the idea of being a teacher in a place like that. I asked her to get me a job, and she did, so off I went to work. There weren't any classrooms; we used adapted buses from the ETC [Empresa de Transportes Colectivos del Estado], the state bus company. These vehicles were of no use to the company anymore, so they adapted them as classrooms for twelve children. There we worked, in the middle of the mud; that winter it even snowed. The children went barefoot, I remember. We had problems with the local people, who thought of us as some sort of authority, and they were used to fighting with the authorities. The children pinched the female teachers' backsides because they wanted to bring them down a peg or two. . . . I felt fine there—I wore thick shoes to work so they didn't think of me as posh.

I had a project I wanted to do at the school . . . I wanted to break with the classical school structure; that is, I wanted to take the school out of the classroom and take it into the country where you could learn from work. The local residents were organized in areas. There was a leadership committee, and each block had a representative on the committee. There were areas: parks and gardens; construction—because there was building going on; education. I belonged to the area of education of the neighborhood (*campamento*); I even thought about going to live there. There was also an area of health—they had a little clinic they had managed to set up themselves. My idea was to take the children to the area of health, for instance, and the personnel of the clinic would give them some lessons—personal hygiene, how your body works, et cetera. I would take them to the building site, and, while they were making paving stones for the streets or whatever, I thought that the children could learn something of geometry, how you need mathematics in carpentry, in a more direct way—well, that was my idea. My colleagues and the ministry all opposed it at first, but later they sort of let me have my own way. It ended very badly and I don't want to talk about it. I worked there for a year. Afterward I was in a very bad way and didn't do anything for a long time.

I separated from my husband. We had been growing further and further apart, I felt that he—politically we agreed in theory, but not in praxis. He told me what I was doing was ridiculous, although I found out later he spoke with pride of what I did. I would arrive home, and he'd start talking about the poetry of the Altiplano [Andean highlands] when what I wanted to talk about was what impressed me of the reality I was working in, my projects. There was more and more distance between us.

[Sonia finally separated from her husband. Later she found another man, the father of her younger daughter, Dora, in the same place where she was then working as a teacher.]

Well, we started to live together. I was so depressed, more than depressed; I had to put my life together again. I read and read and read, four hundred pages a day on average: fiction. I had contact only with children; I lived in a township called La Florida, far away. My ex-husband gave me a very decent monthly allowance, enough to support myself. I didn't even have to work, I didn't have to do anything if I didn't want to. I never went to a psychologist, which is odd. I should have done, but I didn't want to be with adults. My family, on my mother's side, was quite concerned and thought I had turned into a hippie. I just played with the kids in the neighborhood; they came and sang songs with me and made films in my house. I was completely out of it. I was disconnected from the UP [Unidad Popular] period then. I got away from it all. I did my work, followed my interests, but only with children and free of charge. I would make modeling clay in the house, and the kids would come and play with it, making things. I would teach them children's songs, together with other neighborhood women. They looked after the plants and I looked after the kids. My house was always full of children.

I used to see my husband too. There was still a strong relationship, and he would come to see the children and we would talk, something most people found very surprising. We got on very well—Nibaldo, my new companion, Julio, and myself. My ex-husband helped me on many occasions. If I wasn't well, he would take the children with him. Sometimes days would go by and I hardly ate anything; I cried a lot or else I spent my time reading novels—that form of depression.

Then it so happened that Nibaldo was transferred to Viña and we went to live there. It was December 1972. We all moved there. I gave a lot for that relationship. I felt better in Viña, but he didn't get on there. There were lots of problems—the workers, strikes, problems getting building materials . . . he began to get rid of his nervous tension at home, and I realized that he needed psychiatric help. I tried hard to get him to a psychiatrist, a psychologist. I went to a psychologist myself, to make him go, but I couldn't get him attended to. It was the beginning of the end, although we remained together for fourteen years. He had difficulties with the children, he attacked their self-esteem; he competed with my ex-husband in unconventional ways; apparently, he accepted a lot of things about Julio. Although he cared about the children, he would suddenly turn on them in the most awful way. I left him many times because of this, then I would go back, leave, go back, until I finally separated for good about three years ago.

The Coup

While all this was going on, in 1973 I started taking some courses in the Pedagógico of Valparaíso, and then there was the coup . . . I didn't belong to the party anymore; I had left when I was twenty-one, and after my experience in that slum settlement, I distanced myself from all that. I was a sort of fellow traveler, but I kept my distance, I had no active role. I didn't renege on my position as a leftist or Marxist. I don't know if I'd describe myself as a Marxist now, but I still consider myself on the left. Well, I'm studying, the coup takes place, they close the Pedagógico. Then we moved to Santiago, after Nibaldo was detained; I left everything, house, everything just as it was. When Nibaldo was detained I came straight to Santiago with nothing more than a small bag. I didn't go back. We're talking about October 1973—I didn't go back to my house until February 1974. Instead I went to La Florida, to the house that had been left with my brother and his wife, my younger brother, Sandro . . . I haven't told you about his education; he studied philosophy for a year, didn't do well, and studied no more; my other younger brother, Camilo, who has cancer now, worked as a sort of de facto elementary teacher.

Well, my brother gave me back the house in La Florida and I stayed there for a time, and in other houses too. Then Nibaldo was freed but had to go into hiding; I don't know—him in hiding, me going to see him. Here I received help from my mother-in-law, the mother of my first and only husband from the legal point of view. She took the children for a few days. I stayed with her, too, on occasions; other times I stayed with my mother. I felt much less close to my mother than to my mother-in-law, in terms of support. Nibaldo hid with relatives, friends, others who were willing to help him, and I would go to see him to help him; it was a very difficult situation. Finally, a sister of his, who had already left the country, sent him an air ticket to Peru, thinking that from there he could fly to another country. He asked me if I would go with him, and I said, "I'm not leaving, I'm staying," so he didn't leave either. Little by little we came out of hiding. He even dared to start working in La Florida, making furniture at first. Nineteen seventy-four was a very difficult year for us. I started to work as a high school teacher in a school on the outskirts of Santiago. Work was not difficult to find at that time. All it needed was that some philosophy teacher you knew offered you some of his or her hours in some place or other, and you went along and got the job. I had seventeen hours in that school, more or less, and earned very little. . . . I had gone back to the Pedagógico but could take only one course because of the way the courses were organized. In Valparaíso the organization had been different. So the only course I could take in 1974 was statistics—at least I think it was 1974, I can't remember . . . anyway, I started studying again with all these delays. . . . Papers showing I had already passed some courses mysteriously disappeared, some other courses had to be repeated . . . I even had three different curricula. I don't think it was chance that lost those papers for me; they wanted to make life difficult for those of us who had been a markedly Marxist generation; it just made me more determined. The more difficulties I encountered, the more determined and stubborn I became.

So, I finally graduated in 1976, expecting a baby too—that was Dora, who's now twelve. Dora was born in 1976, and the same year I had more or less fulfilled all the requirements to get my degree. . . . It was the longest undergraduate education in history, even if you only counted the years I had studied in a regular fashion. I had been at it for more years than the degree normally required, although it wasn't because I'd ever had to repeat any courses. In 1976 I finished absolutely everything, practical requirements, everything. I didn't get my degree, though, until 1978. By that time I was working in a school here in Santiago. I had got a transfer from the other one. Or maybe it wasn't a transfer, perhaps I just registered one of my children there, and when they realized I taught philosophy they offered me some hours. I was lucky in that I had not been politically active during the UP period, otherwise I wouldn't have got the job. . . . I can't remember how much I earned, but it wasn't much, because I taught only a few hours.

I had the allowance from my ex-husband, which as I said was a fair amount—until he was thrown out of the university. He then went off to a provincial university but was fired again—for political reasons, obviously. At first he gave me the money from the sale of the house he had inherited; later it was my mother-in-law who gave me the allowance—something she has done up to this day. However, if at one time the amount would have paid the rent of a house, now it doesn't even pay a quarter of a rent. It's only 10,500 pesos. However, my mother-in-law later started paying an allowance to my son, who is studying in the provinces, and buys him some clothing from time to time. At the moment Julio gives our daughter a sort of allowance . . . that is, Julio doesn't give me money anymore, my mother-in-law does that, but he gives the child money for photocopies, her lunch, things like that. I'm not sure where Julio works right now; I know he's involved in research of some sort and has had quite a difficult time financially. I don't know what his current situation is, neither am I particularly interested. We have practically no relationship anymore. He has another wife; they have two children and live in their own house, which her father gave her. They get help from her parents . . . that is, they have an easier time than I do. In fact my children are very critical of the situation; they compare what they eat in their father's house with what they eat at home, for example. But those things don't bother me anymore.

Nibaldo started a company of his own—he's very creative—painting buildings and getting it done very quickly; he even does redecoration. He's also worked in wood for this or that firm and for a lumberyard—he has tended toward that field. He studied both engineering and architecture, but graduated in neither. We separated around 1984. I felt pretty good afterward—as if a heavy load had been taken off my shoulders—our relationship had been such a difficult one.

The Employment Merry-Go-Round

All those years I continued working as a teacher, but . . . I had so many changes. Everything is mixed up with illness and other problems. For example, in 1980 I had kidney tuberculosis, so I was a year off work, on sick leave, not working but being paid all the same. I was registered in the old system of social security at the time . . . so I didn't work and was paid by the social security institute.

When I went back to work, the Ministerio de Educación had adopted its monetary criteria, and decided I should divide my schedule, which had increased in the meantime. I was in charge of the Department of Counseling—specifically I was head of performance; that is, I monitored all the pupils, supervised their performance, and counseled the kids with problems. Well, they decided this was a luxury, and so they divided my time between two high schools, the one I was already in and another one. After my illness, I found this rather heavy going. Then Dora became deaf—she went deaf at eleven months, in 1977. I lived a long way from my work, in Macul again. I had to take Dora every day to her special school and also attend the school for parents, which was obligatory. At the time I was separated, in fact I was nearly always separated from Nibaldo for reasons of work—he had to work in the South for various reasons. I couldn't manage with the two schools. . . .

Everybody was very alarmed by municipalization. You arrived at a school and found everybody panic-stricken. "We're going to be fired," or "what's going on at the ministry?" I was quite happy in the commercial institute [Sonia had found full-time employment in one place], and the pupils liked me too—sufficient reason for mistrust [on the authorities' part]. So half of my schedule was transferred, because the institute was no longer municipal. The commercial schools were taken over by some other agency, I don't remember [what one]. So my schedule was divided once again, this time between two commercial schools.

I persisted and found myself a post in another commercial school where I could have a full schedule in one place. I was very happy there, until they changed all the last grades that I taught to an evening schedule so I wasn't free until 8:30 P.M. and thus arrived home at 9:30 P.M. and didn't see my children because they were all in bed asleep. They went to school in the mornings, and I worked in the afternoons.

I was living in the Recoleta neighborhood at the time, so I asked for a transfer to a high school in that neighborhood that was relatively close to home, and where I could work mornings and then have some time with my children. I was there when municipalization was implemented. We went out on strike. I was active in the strike; we were very involved, and the school was the one which lasted longest on strike. But I had a sort of image because the students looked up to me a lot. They then had the idea of transforming the philosophy program and introducing two semesters of moral philosophy. Perhaps they thought we might give sermons, and the pupils would think less. I tried to make the classes more entertaining, using reality, the moral problems of the pupils themselves . . . so I was accused of talking politics in class, because certain words were used in my classes, such as unemployment, democracy, freedom. I began to have trouble with the principal. It wasn't important, but then the strike turned me into a figure, someone who had given entertaining classes and thus had influence among the pupils. I was dangerous and was one of those fired. That was February 1987.

I have worked in lots of different schools. In one of them I had a free-lance contract to do workshops. I began to work on improving teaching skills. Before I lost my job, I had the salary of a high school teacher, 45,000 pesos, and with one thing and another I made another 20,000. I lived on that and the 10,000 odd from my mother-in-law. . . .

Three years ago I moved to this apartment, after I separated from Nibaldo. And after the earthquake we had in Chile, the house I was living in then was a bit damaged, and I was rather nervous as I thought it might collapse. By that time my life had changed; I couldn't afford a maid, I lived in a house with a backyard, a garden, the garbage had to be thrown out, et cetera, et cetera, so I moved to this apartment, thinking my mother is here two floors below. If I didn't have a maid, she could at least keep an eye out for my daughter. She owns her apartment now, since 1981. But when I moved in the rent was about 14,000 pesos; today it's 50,000, 55,000, just the rent. On top of that you have to add the shared expenses like hot water, which is very expensive. A friend passed the apartment on to me, but after I became unemployed I had problems paying the rent. I never left off paying though; once I was late paying and that was the reason for the court case. I lost the case and now I have to leave. I have appealed and am now waiting for the decision.

When I became unemployed, everyone thought I would go to live with my mother. Then one of my uncles, one of my mother's brothers, lived with my mother and so did my brother; the three of them lived together. The uncle left because he thought I had no option but to move in with my mother, and my brother got married, so now my poor mother lives on her own and gets very depressed. But I'm not going to live with her, even though the alternative is to live in a shed. I love her very much but I have my own life, my children are accustomed to a different life-style. My mother is very organized and has life rather programmed, so I prefer not to live with her. My mother retired as a school principal and has a widow's pension too; she also has a second pension as a teacher because she went back to work after retiring as principal. She lives off that income. She also administered this building for many years, so that was further income for her in the past, but now she hasn't got that anymore. She receives about 90,000 pesos a month, which allows her to live well as long as she doesn't get upset, and stops spending so much money buying meat. What I mean is that she's a bit alarmed because it's the first time she's been without my uncle's salary and my brother's salary too, and she thinks she won't be able to manage. But she owns the apartment, so there's no mortgage to pay, so with 90,000 she can live perfectly well. She's still getting used to it though. She doesn't help me. I only get help from Julio's mother with the 10,500 pesos, and Nibaldo . . . well, since I was fired he sometimes sends me something, but I haven't had anything from him now since September. He started sending me 50,000, 40,000, 30,000—I've got it noted down—20,000, 80,000. He had said he would send 100,000, but really I haven't received that much. He lives in Chiloé now and has a new family and a newborn baby girl.

Well, last year I was fired. I went round a few subsidized schools for girls—they were all dreadful places. Last year I was fired three times. First, I was dismissed from the public high school; then I went to a school where they paid me very badly, something like 17,000 pesos; and then I taught in a convent school, which was not so terrible but I had trouble adapting to the religious environment. They paid me 30,000 pesos, so I did the two jobs. Later an acquaintance offered me a job at her school for a salary of 45,000, so I resigned from one of the schools, stayed on in the convent school where I [taught] fifteen hours, and took the job with thirty hours at the new school. That way my income add[ed] up to 75,000. I could have taken forty hours at the new school, but I already had fifteen at the convent school and didn't want to resign. So I [had] forty-five hours of work a week, plus the further education for teachers that I have always carried on with and for which I [got] paid a fee; you get paid when—but I'll save talking about that for later: my tale of "pedagogical renewal." . . .

I still hadn't asked Nibaldo for help. Together with the other extra odds and ends that I got from my teaching skills courses, I thought that the 75,000 would be enough to live on. I didn't have a maid, so I had to do the house and the two jobs and look after all the counseling in one of the schools. Then they sent me to an industrial school too, which belonged to them as well, but that was just too much. I spoke to the owner of the school and told her I just couldn't do so much. She suggested I come and work full-time in her school. I had many doubts because I could see that it was a school where they sometimes didn't pay the water bill; they lied—they would inaugurate the computer room here today and then tomorrow take all the equipment and inaugurate it in another of their schools. I could see that this woman was a bit odd, a little bit mad, but I never imagined she'd do what she did to me. So I resigned from the convent school, pressured by circumstances and by the fact that my income from there was the smaller of the two, and accepted her offer. A week later I was fired. Why? Because they had money troubles. The owner was quite mad; the accountant took charge of everything and told me that they had to cut back on everything that was a luxury, and that counseling fell into that category. From one day to the next, without warning, without anything, on a day I was hanging my own curtains in the counseling room, I was thrown out. They gave me a month's salary, and the very same day I took my things and left. That was in May 1987, I think.

Surviving Unemployment

That whole experience left me deeply depressed; it was the first time I had felt that way after being fired. The other times had not affected me so much. I told myself, "You have to survive, you can't just be a teacher," but that was my place in the world and it really got to me. Then it got mixed up with sentimental problems, and I guess also problems of regression. Nibaldo would say to me, "Sonita, how are you?" and I would answer, "I don't feel at all good." I don't actually remember if it happened on this occasion that I lost my job or the third time I was sacked that he invited me to spend a few days with him at a spa, and I went. So, on top of everything else, the situation was complicated by a series of reencounters. I think it must have been after the third time I was fired that he took me to the spa.

That third time was like this: there was a woman who owned a well-known school in Las Condes—there is evidence of what I am saying—I've come to the conclusion that if you have serious psychiatric problems and a bit of money that you don't know what to do with, you start a school. I've come across so many crazy people. . . . It happened like this: a friend called me and said, "Sonia, I'm going to give up my counseling hours in such-and-such a school." Why didn't she warn me? I was desperate and went along and took on the hours, although I did realize that the old lady was a bit odd, but she was going to pay me 45,000 pesos for three days' work. A week later, she was already trying to go back on all our agreements, saying that she couldn't pay my social security, that it would be better if I worked for a fee, not a salary, and so on. . . . Two weeks later she sacked me. She decided she couldn't really afford the expense. That was my third expulsion from the system, and it left me feeling really low—I think that was when I went to the spa—well, I never actually got to the spa, Nibaldo was separating from the woman he had lived a year with in the South, and we ended up back together again, a situation that dragged miserably on until very recently. I suppose the problem was that I needed to feel protected. But the cure was worse than the illness; what happened was I ended up going back and forth from the South, with the relationship getting worse all the time. By that time he had another daughter by the other woman and he was all mixed up by the situation, apparently suffering a great deal.

Dianita—our daughter—lived through the whole episode. Her father would come to see me, and we lived like a family for three or four days, and then I went south. Later I would even let Diana visit his house in Chiloé, something I didn't want to do at first, but then I said, "Okay, let her go." So she went to be there for her sister's birth and came back when the baby was three months old. And my situation . . .

I have so many debts. . . . Now I am working in a dance studio (I do psychology of learning and counseling) and earn 30,000 pesos, which goes straight to pay the rent—I'm left with nothing. Well, I've got the 10,000 from my mother-in-law; I do the teacher skills training, but they pay me badly, and late or never. I do a few hours of drama games in a school where they pay me less than 5,000 pesos. I do two hours of drama games a week. I was conducting a workshop on anger and guilt in a feminist center. I got about 10,000 pesos a month for that, but I did it for two months and they still haven't paid me for the last one.

What to do? . . . I don't usually turn to people for help. I invent something new. I don't get help from . . . that is, if I have problems, suppose I can't pay the rent, but I know that the day after tomorrow I will have the money, then my mother lends me the money and a couple of days later I pay it back to her. One of my brothers once helped me to set myself up selling clothes (last year I sold clothes). My brother lent me 30,000 pesos, and I bought sweatshirts and sold them at a profit and paid him back little by little. Then when I still had 15,000 to pay, he said "forget it"; but I gave him an armchair—he got married and I gave him an armchair that I had. It's the way I am, I have great difficulty accepting help. Furthermore, all my brothers are badly off; there's no one in the family who can comfortably help me. Many of my cousins are out of work; my family is a family of teachers, what more can I say? . . .

Let's see, I do have girlfriends who come to see me; very few of them have money. One of them who is better off would buy a sweater from me to help me. It cost me 2,500 pesos and I sold it for 5,000. I started taking my wares to offices. At the beginning I organized meetings here and sold clothes. I'm good at putting on shows, so I organized something a bit special here—like "try on what you fancy." After that I sold books, last year too. I found that it was easier to sell clothes than books. If I offer someone a book on Greek culture that costs 4,500 pesos, they'll say, "How nice, how expensive"; if I offer them a sweater for the same price, they'll say "how nice" and buy it. So I sold clothes.

I have also done workshops; let's see, this year in March I went north and organized a workshop for training mental health monitors. They paid me 40,000 pesos for two days. I get that sort of job through friends, although people get to hear good things about my workshops too. In January I did two teacher skills improvement training courses; one was on drama games for beginners and the other was on the handling of values and feelings in the classroom. For that I got 70,000 pesos all at once. These are courses for schoolteachers. Last year, for instance, I went to quite an important school here in Santiago and did a two-session workshop on the critical analysis of practice. They paid me 7,500 pesos per session, and the extra money was welcome at Christmas time.

I do these courses all the year round; there are four periods in all. I used to earn a lot more but now the Colegio de Profesores has a different policy and sends the teachers to the comunas, and there we get paid badly, and late or never. It's different, too, because you can't get the same number of people together as you could when it was centralized. Sometimes you've only got five or six pupils now. You can't have a workshop with less than twenty people, but out in the communes, since the local people pay, you have to do it. There are fewer workshops altogether as well. Let's say that the year before last, last year, I sometimes ran two or three parallel workshops a week; that gave me a higher income on the one hand, and, on the other, more pupils. There had to be sixty pupils at least—twenty, twenty, and twenty. Now the numbers are far lower. Well, I try to manage but sometimes we simply don't have . . . it's not that we can't eat; sometimes we're short, but we've never had to eat really badly.

My two older children are studying in the university. We don't pay anything for the tuition because I keep on at the social workers until I get 100 percent scholarships . . . well, they're loans now. One day they'll have to be paid. Actually my daughter doesn't get 100 percent, she gets 86 percent. Either her grandmother or her father pays the difference, which is around 3,000 pesos. Last year she had a scholarship of 45 percent, from the Universidad Católica, plus a 45 percent loan, so 10 percent was left over to be paid.

Vacations—well, this year we went to the beach. My younger brother invited us along. He rented a house and invited me with the woman he is now married to; at the time she was just his girlfriend. I paid for the food, nothing else, and he rented the house. That is the help I have received. And sometimes, suddenly, like when I was faced with the court case about the overdue rent, and I thought I was going to be in trouble, I realized that I had a great ability to obtain money, if I wanted to. I asked a girlfriend for 20,000 pesos, and she lent it to me and has not let me pay her back. A cousin lent me 20,000; I've paid 10,000 and still owe him 10,000. Another girlfriend lent me 20,000 pesos, and I've paid her back. My friend whom I didn't pay back because she said she didn't need it—one day she said she would have me pay her some way, and I know she's a good friend; probably the other one didn't need the money either, but she's not such a good friend, and I paid her back.

I have many friends; the profession has brought me many of them, through the daily contact. If I have a problem, I tell my friends, not my family. Of course, if I need urgent help, my family is always prepared to help me. It's a system that's been established de facto; we help each other mutually—for instance, I will hand on clothing that my children have grown out of to my nephew, and my sister-in-law will sew things for me free of charge. The relationship with the cousins is more distant, with the exception of one cousin whom I know I can always count on. I hardly ever see my father's family, except for a female cousin that I get on with very well. But it would never occur to me to ask her for a cent, never. She even knows that I have financial difficulties, but she's never offered to help. You can see if you come to my home that we lack things, but I've never received anything from the part of my family that's better off than I am.

I think that I'm a special case too. It's not that I don't accept help. I do accept help; if someone comes and says, "Look, I've got this lamp, would you like to have it?" I would accept it. But I don't think I project an image of a person who can't manage, in spite of the fact that those who know me well know that I have bad times in that sense, but they are used to seeing Sonia fall down and then get up again. So I suppose they don't think to offer help. Besides, we have simple tastes here in my home. The people that visit us are similar, and we don't worry much about unnecessary things. With regard to food, I actually think that families that are better off than ours, with more-stable salaries, don't eat as well as we do, because the desire to save or to put on a certain appearance socially makes people sometimes tighten their belts where the quality of their meals is concerned. I don't do that. We eat relatively well; no luxuries, but every day there's milk in the house, we eat beef, eggs.

Now I've got this problem of the apartment. I've got to leave and I don't know what I'm going to do. I really don't know. The judge said that I have to come to some arrangement and hand over the house in September. I told her I couldn't. "But you must." I shrugged my shoulders and replied, "I can't." "Well, when can you leave?" "I don't know"; I said I would commit myself to leaving next January, but they wouldn't accept that. I did not give in. So all I can say is that I don't know. Between now and January I think I can sort something out.

Friendship in Action

I feel I have very good friendships, and I think that, given the poverty of my, let's say, economic existence, people must like me for other reasons, there's no doubt about it. They always offer me support. . . . I remember when I was unemployed—I was laid off in February 1987 when masses of teachers were fired. At first I looked for work; I have already told you how I got on, I went round looking and then decided that I didn't want a boss anymore and that I would do something else. I don't remember which came first, selling clothes or selling books, but I ended up selling clothes. It was one of my brothers that lent me the money—I didn't actually need a lot—about 40,000 pesos. I paid the money off in comfortable instalments up until recently, [when,] as I told you, I gave him an armchair. I noticed that some of my friends bought clothes from me because they needed them, some bought because they needed them and also wanted to help me, and yet others clearly wanted to buy something from me at all costs; they searched through what I had until they found something that more or less suited them or somebody else, just as long as they bought something from me. Another thing that happened, for instance: a friend called Fanny would buy something and give me more than the price of the garment, and say, "Keep the change, we'll take it off the next thing I buy from you." But it was a way of helping me. There are different attitudes among the people that have helped me. There are some that I know I have to pay back because our relationship depends on it. There's a different attitude—you can see that it hurts them to lend.

I have very rarely asked for money in my life, but once when I was really stuck, my mother got on the telephone and called. She called a friend and a cousin. My cousin lent me the money without establishing any conditions as to how or when I was to pay him back; the friend also, but I noticed that she was not comfortable with the open-ended arrangement, and I paid her back as soon as I could. In contrast, I have another friend with a completely different attitude, an attitude of true affection and support and a recognition of the fact that money is nothing compared with other things that we have. Well, as far as economic aid is concerned, that is the most I've ever had; once three people lent me about 60,000 pesos. I've paid it all back except the part my friend Fanny lent me.

Reciprocity

Well, I've always helped people myself—one of the reasons I haven't a cent. I've got a friend who's always been worse off than I am, no matter how badly off I was. I think a lot of him. He's not young; he's a worker with an exceptional cultural level who ended up selling books. He's also a rebel, maladjusted, let's say, and I know that he has serious problems, very severe problems. I've always helped him. He's one of the people that I've helped—well, I don't really like the word *help,* it sounds like granting favors. I've never expected him to give me anything in return. It doesn't even feel like help. I don't like talking about help. It just feels natural, not like a favor. When you do someone a favor, you're conscious that you're doing a favor; when one uses the word *help* it's like—it reminds me a bit of the idea of charity. This is a case of solidarity, which is different. So he sells books, this friend. Sometimes you don't really need books but he comes and you buy; sometimes you know you can buy the same book elsewhere much cheaper, but that's different. This is a form of help. I would say that I have this sort of relationship with just about everyone—my relatives, close friends—peso bills go in both directions.

But there is a certain type of person that I don't want to help. I don't quite know how to define them, but they are people, for instance, that have a sort of submissive mentality—like a servant or something. Then you're not helping an equal. I don't like help when it's not between equals. In contrast, for example, this friend of mine who was a worker—he doesn't have a university education, he's self-taught, and as regards his origins, he's not my equal. But now, his present education, his posture . . .

Let's see, another type of help is when you need a doctor. In that case the help is in a different form, as I have a cousin with a private practice. For example, she sees to my children. Usually, because I want to maintain my freedom, and receiving favors can make you dependent on certain types of people, I nearly always end up paying for the appointments. But sometimes she doesn't let me. I will sometimes pay her three visits with a health-care check or two. She will accept those. But, for example, she's just moved to a house near here and I lent her a piece of furniture for her kitchen. This type of favor is typical in the environment I move in. That is, she hasn't the money to buy the piece of furniture, I've got one put away, so I lend it to her.

Perpetual Restlessness: Marcia Vidal

My parents aren't from Santiago; they come from a small town in the Fifth Region [Quinta Región]. They moved to Santiago after getting married; then they went back to live in the provinces, and all their children were born there. My father was a public employee at the time. My mother was a dressmaker here in Santiago, once they came back.

We lived in Nuñoa. Then, in 1973 there was the military coup, and my father lost his job. He belonged to a political party, and, well, they fired him because of the project he was involved in; all the people on the project were fired. He was out of work for a long time, and for a while during this period my parents went back to their hometown, taking just me with them. My three brothers and sisters remained in Santiago. There are four of us altogether.

After my father lost his job, we lived on what my mother earned. . . . We had a lot of difficulties because my brothers and sisters were leaving school and couldn't go on to university, or else they were admitted to university in another part of Chile and my parents couldn't afford the expense. Then, my sister paid for her education herself, by knitting and selling socks and sweaters. She studied and worked to pay for her university education. I was in private school at that time. Then, when we went back to Santiago, I went to a public school.

Finally, in 1976, my father found a permanent job. He had not studied anything, he didn't have a profession. But he had the experience of his previous work and had some knowledge of accounting.

I finished school and started studying pedagogy in a private institute. My sister finished her university education and got married. Financially, she was completely independent from us—in fact she had been so since she started university. One of my brothers finished high school and studied something to do with the textile industry. But he too was out of work because the factories began to go bankrupt, and so there was no work for him. He started selling things, glasses, all kinds of things. He lived with us until he got married and left home. He carried on as a salesman, the same as before. My other brother, the one who comes just before me in the family, started courses on several different subjects but didn't finish any of them. He had to get married too, and my father bought him a farm, so now he's a farmer. Well, later all their lives changed. . . .

We lived in Nuñoa, in an apartment at first and later in a house. My parents sold the house and gave part of the money to my brother who had done the textile course so he could start a business. Now he's got a small company making laboratory instruments. He also imports and sells them. This development changed his life. I don't know if he's a rich man, but he's certainly better off than when he was just a salesman. My other brother, the farmer, had to work very hard. It took him five years of hard work, because he has a plantation of trees that had to mature. Only recently has he been able to relax a bit. He had to come to Santiago to study; then his wife wanted to study photography and now works as a photographer here; they have a place here too. That is, they live here and on the farm really. She's getting on very well in her work. She works in television. And my brother is still a farmer.

As for me, well I studied basic pedagogy for four years in the private institute; five years being supported by my parents. Then I started working when I was in the final year of the course. It happened that the teacher I had as a tutor had cancer. She had recently been operated on so she let me have her class, and she was such a nice person that she paid me out of her own salary. So I had paid teaching practice and at the end kept the course in the school. It was an Adventist school. I couldn't stay there for long because I didn't belong to that church, which was a requirement for working there. But I did work there during that year. Furthermore, it was a school that paid very well, because they paid me by the hour. It was subsidized. I worked there all the year before last. Afterward, last year, while I did my final paper before qualifying, I got a job in a subsidized school. I earned 15,000 pesos a month there, which was the average salary for all teachers. In other words, I started out earning the same as everyone else working there. Thirty hours a week; they didn't pay any overtime there, just your salary and that was all.

This year I worked in the Summer School organized by the Colegio de Profesores, and one of the people I met had just been made principal of a school and needed someone to fill a vacancy and told me to apply. So I did, because I was looking for a job that paid a bit better. I got the job and there I get 30,000 pesos net for about twenty-five hours. That's where I'm working now. This school also pays overtime; it's got a different policy, it's one of those schools practicing what they call alternative education. So they pay overtime, and the work is organized in areas. I'm in charge of one of the areas. It's a middle-class school. All the parents have a profession, but they are middle class, that is, there isn't anyone you'd call upper class. The school is located in a comuna in the southeast of Santiago. It doesn't have a lot of pupils, which means the school's income is not large either.

Well, that's what I'm doing at the moment, apart from a million other things that don't earn me money. I'm in a study group, a group of teachers who get together to study. We meet here. All the other members of the group had more experience than I had; they give courses and other things like that, so when we planned the year's activities the director said I was to work with him on the workshops, since I was new in the group (and new as a teacher—I didn't give courses or anything). He said that way I could learn to coordinate, which would be useful later on when the TED [Talleres de Educación Democrática, or Democratic Education Workshops] got started, as I would have the necessary experience. Well, we've been working on the preparation of this month's event. I've got some projects in the school that I hope will get funding if we get good results this year.

Basically I have the one job, which occupies me every morning and two afternoons a week. I don't live with my parents anymore. A year ago I left home and became independent. Well, I don't know if I should really call it independence, because what happened was that my father had an apartment, which used to belong to my sister when she got married. My father practically gave it to me as a gift, because the mortgage payment is something like 35,000 a month, so my only real possibility of being truly independent is sharing with another person. I couldn't manage on my own. So the agreement is that I live with one of my cousins, who is also financially supported by my father. My cousin doesn't have a father, and studies here. He is not from Santiago. So I support him, and in exchange, my father pays the mortgage.

I can't really called myself independent. With my salary—well, I promised my father that I would save 5,000 pesos a month in order to pay off something of the apartment loan at the end of the year. But I haven't been able to do it, I just don't have enough. My 30,000 pesos only just enable me to pay gas, electricity, maintenance, food, et cetera, but I can't save anything, nothing at all. . . . Transportation costs me 8,000 pesos—that's what I spend most on. I take the bus to school, there and back, that's two bus journeys, but I have so many other things to do and meetings to attend that I have to take some form of transport several times a day. On occasions I spend up to 1,000 pesos in a day just on buses. I sometimes ask for time off from school to go to a meeting in another place, so I have to take a bus to get there and then another to get back to the school, then I have to go off somewhere else. So transportation costs add up, although I walk a lot, but when you're in a hurry you can't always be walking everywhere.

My colleagues—well, I think the men have more problems. Usually husband and wife both work and only just manage to survive, always having to ask for advances or borrow money, getting into debt one way or another. The women, at least from what I see at my school, are lucky enough to have husbands that earn more or less well, that is, the wife's salary is like a sort of extra. [Even with two working teachers in a family, economic strains can be overwhelming. Marcia's boyfriend, also a teacher, saw his first marriage fail. He and his first wife] both worked in subsidized schools where the salaries are not usually more than 20,000 pesos, and they were paying rent, et cetera. Now he wants to study something different and do other things too, because he had to go back to live with his parents. . . . He hasn't got any children. They were married for a very short time.

We have talked about living together many times, but it would be impossible even though I earn more than he does. He has some hours of teaching and in one of the schools he works in he gets 17,000 and 4,000 pesos in the other. If you add both our incomes together, we could manage but we couldn't continue studying—I'd like to study some more too. There wouldn't be enough for that. He wouldn't be able to get a government loan *[crédito fiscal]* for university studies because he is already a graduate and what's more, he owes money to the university. If we went on living here, one of us could study, but the other would have to wait until the first had finished. What I want to study is very expensive. I want to do a master's in learning problems at the Universidad Católica. That costs US $750 a year, this year, apart from books and other things you have to buy.

I hope to be able to finance my master's; I want to save up so I'm doing some credits in the school to see if next year they'll give me a raise, and perhaps I'll be able to get more work in my free time and then start to save. I've no other option because there aren't any scholarships. Well, there are grants, but hardly any and I can't count on getting one. My boyfriend wants to study law or to carry on studying pedagogy; but pedagogy, for instance, in history, which would be better in that there are more history classes in schools than French, which is what he teaches right now—French is an optional subject; this means that he has to study about four years, practically all within the speciality. I don't know how much the Universidad Metropolitana is charging right now, but he is considering the alternative of another institute, where graduates pay 50 percent less. That would come out to around 8,000 pesos.

At any rate we can't live together because his family supports him economically, and practically all he earns he saves for his future studies. Well, I live away from my parents—it was an idea I had a long time ago, a need to survive on my own, although they do pay the mortgage so I'm not so alone as all that . . . but living on 30,000 pesos. . . . When I lived with my parents, 30,000 was a lot of money for someone like me. I saved money then, I could buy myself clothes, books, I could go out on the weekends, and so forth. But not now; I've got a responsibility that comes before all those other things; I've sort of left them behind. Sometimes I feel anxious about it all.

I suddenly think about having children; I want to have children and I calculate how much it would cost. Having a child today—I don't know how I would do it with what I earn and what Mariano earns . . . all the ideas you have as a teacher for your own children . . . you want to have them in a good school, a good kindergarten. There are dreams that you have that you know will never come true if we go on the way we are now. . . . A couple like us, even if we didn't have these plans to study more, if we had to pay rent, it would be the end. There are still quite a number of years before he finishes with his studies. Life is really very difficult for a young couple without the help of their parents or of someone who can lend them an apartment or something, because even if they got together to pay a rent, they would hardly have enough even for that. From my experience and what I've seen, nobody escapes the help of their parents. Very few people can live at this level unless they live with someone who earns a lot of money—well, around 100,000 pesos, which isn't so much, but enough to rent something decent and live with the two incomes added together. If I were completely on my own, I couldn't do it. And from what I've seen—I've got colleagues who have been married two years, living together, and then have had to live separately for three years, each one in his or her parents' home, until they find better jobs; and then they can go back to living together again only with great difficulty. The other option is just to separate—a bit like going back to dating.

It's very discouraging with respect to the teaching profession, because you also feel—what I mean is you are a professional just like any other professional and you work as hard as the other person, so why such a low salary? It's really incredible; to earn a decent salary you have to work all day or get a job in a very good school, with a good level of education. There are no other options.

At least I don't have to pay rent. I haven't much in the way of furniture yet. Well, there's my bed, the one I had in my parents' house. They also gave me a kitchen stove and a refrigerator, because once I was going to get married. We had bought a really old stove, and I gave it to my brother to look after for me, the one who lives in the country; he has a farmhand that lives with him who got the stove. So I lost my stove, and then I didn't get married, and time went by; then they gave me another stove. I also had a very old refrigerator, but my brother used that to store the dog food, so it had got very knocked about—you had to kick it shut, it was on its last legs. It didn't come back to Santiago either, so I was given another one. What else? I don't have a sofa or living room furniture; I've got a dining table and chairs, also a gift, and that's all.

My cousin who lives with me studies and doesn't work. My father gives him a bit of money so I make him responsible for one of the bills, the electricity, for example, or he has to buy the bread. I can't afford the bread, so we buy just enough bread, and anyway he eats more bread than I do, because I'm hardly ever at home. I just come in at night and eat something. Usually I cook myself something, more than eat bread—bread's more something he needs.

For my generation it's difficult to begin a life as a couple. Usually no one intends to live with their parents or parents-in-law. At first they go off together alone and rent a room or something way out on the outskirts of town—very cheap. But it always ends up in difficulties and there's never enough money. So, they try going back to one of the parents' homes. Whoever is the in-law has the worst time of it because it's not really his or her family, and you feel you have to be—well, what I mean is, you can't have a fight with your partner or anything. What happens is that the parents continue to handle one's life as they see fit, and really they have every right because the couple is in their house—even if all they occupy is a bedroom. Now if there are children, it's much worse. There's the question of not being able to send them to the play group or the kindergarten because that costs money. Better they should go to grandma, and then there are problems with grandma. Dependency of this type always has a very high cost. But it is inevitable, because the change is usually very sharp . . . for example, in my case, from living quite well to changing your whole life-style from one day to the next. It's very sudden. Then you either get desperate or you just get on with getting used to it.

I have a commitment to my parents about the apartment. I don't say I would never move back with them, I couldn't say that, you never know, but I hope I won't have to do it. Of course it's difficult. And it's more difficult to save in order to carry on studying. The thing is that if I get another job in the afternoons, I won't be able to do any of the things I most like to do, like working with the study group, or the projects. There is a chance that eventually they will lead to something else, that is, we could submit a project to a foreign agency and they might accept it. But if all your time is filled with work, you have no time for anything else of that sort. The present possibilities of financial aid are limited; there are a very few scholarships and the reduction in fees is minimal.

I have good luck with jobs. I'm never short of job opportunities. However, in a municipalized school I would earn the same as I'm getting now, but in very different conditions. . . . Given those working conditions, and earning the same . . .

I wrote my thesis on academic performance, that is, on the influence of the teacher on the pupils' performance. We did the field work in a comuna where there was apparently a good academic level; I say apparently because we found that this was not the case. Our results were not publicized, as this was supposed to be one of the best comunas in the country as far as academic performance was concerned. We did our interviewing just in subsidized schools, where the conditions were appalling. We found out something of the living conditions of the teachers—although we didn't have any items in our questionnaire about this. We made the odd comment on the subject, and the responses allowed us to infer a little about the teachers' situation. We interviewed elementary school teachers. Most of them worked in two schools, and the majority were married with children, so . . .

The questionnaire did include an item on how many schools the interviewee worked for. There were some that worked in three; they taught in the morning, afternoon, and in the evening, literally all day. We also asked about the opportunities for further study. None of them had a postgraduate degree; the most any of them had was the odd short course of some sort that the school had required them to do. Nobody had had the opportunity to study. The questions were very brief, such as "number of courses taken," "have you a postgraduate degree," et cetera. But we did take the opportunity to ask them why they had no further educational qualifications; weren't they interested? The responses indicated that it was basically a matter of money, which led finally to a loss of interest. The years went by without their doing any further study, and that was that. Most of them lived in rented accommodations, either subsidized or belonging to a relative. Hardly anyone was the legal owner of his home.

We were very surprised to find that they didn't acknowledge the low level. We said as much in our viva voce final examination at the Universidad Católica. Our study was a piece of work for the OAS [Organization of American States]. The true situation couldn't be publicly recognized because the comuna we had studied was considered to be one of the best in Chile as regards academic performance. The teachers said that; of course, the PER [Pupil Performance Test] tells us that there is a very high level here. However, they were aware of the fact that if the children don't eat well, if the classrooms are in bad condition, if the atmosphere offered by the school as a whole is unsatisfactory, it's not likely that academic performance will be good, or that the teaching will be good either. Perhaps the requirements are lowered and in that way the children can appear to have a high level, but that probably has little to do with what one expects children to achieve in those grades. The PER data referred to the fourth grade (they have an evaluation now with a different name). Of course, they had good marks, good overall averages, but the real level was extremely low. What one might expect from a child in the second or third grade was being achieved in the fourth grade. It was not difficult to get good results doing things like that. Furthermore, although these tests are supposed to be absolutely anonymous, not even the name of the school is supposed to be known, the teachers were not confident that this was in fact the case. The ideal test would be that the children receive no special preparation and one day they are given the exam, and they do it with whatever knowledge they have. But the teachers know what is going to be tested, and they prepare the children just like they do for the Prueba de Aptitud Académica [for university admission]. So the child is very familiar with what he has to know for the exam. The evaluation loses reliability.

All this is related to the training of the teachers and their conditions. As a teacher, your chances of finding a job depend on where you studied. Generally speaking, if you are measured in terms of professional ability or quality, you have fewer opportunities if you studied in an institute. . . . And also there is the fact that the institutes came into being under the military regime and are just commercial enterprises. Of course, that's true, but the people doing the hiring don't really know whether the training [the institutes] have given us is any good or not. . . . Precisely because the institutes are so new and have to compete for their place in the market, they make heavy demands on their students, in order to prove that they can turn out good professionals. They often demand more than some universities; not all of them though, the Universidad Católica is as good as it ever was.

In my case, basic pedagogy in my institute was different, because we had to take our examinations at the Universidad Católica, which demands a very high level of achievement. The pass level was the highest, class attendance percentages were the highest, everything was the highest. In our first year we were examined by the Universidad de La Serena [in the north of Chile], which was a cinch. In other words, we all passed ten subjects at a time, no problem. But in the second year, with the Universidad Católica, it was a different story; that's when we began to fail some exams. . . . I failed one exam only, but there we all started to have more difficulty in getting through because the level is very high.

You can also appreciate the level of teaching by looking at another aspect, apart from training. There is a basic issue, that is, the constant concern to go on improving one's skills and knowledge. I don't know if it's the same with all professions, but this one fosters a desire to study and to keep on studying, because otherwise you're no good. For example, if you are an elementary school teacher, unless you're in a very good school, you earn 30,000 pesos working all day; you're not doing it for the money. That is, you either have a vocation to teach or you get out. . . .

I feel in some cases there is a difference between our generation and the teachers who were trained before. It's something to do with efficiency . . . I don't know if it's because of the enthusiasm you have when you're newly graduated, or because of the particular environment one moves in, but I see many things that can be done in the profession, especially in the school I work in, which is an open school. In fact it's like an open door; there's also the opportunity to try something new. The older teachers don't seem to question themselves; perhaps they're just too overwhelmed with trying to do other things that they have no time for it. Perhaps we will be the same in a few years' time, I don't know, but I do feel they are different in this sense. We have even talked a lot with the principal about this; he is also upset by this lack of professional feeling on the part of the teachers, despite the fact they work in a private school with relatively good salaries compared with other schools and that they are actually given the chance to work—because they couldn't work as teachers in other schools. They don't take advantage of the situation they enjoy.

Besides, I get the impression that life used to be easier for teachers, the cost of living was lower, and also many teachers, for example, went out into rural areas where they played a very important role in the place they worked. They still do it, but personally I wouldn't go for that. Leaving, isolating myself from everything would be like cutting off my hands. My study group is like nonstop learning for me. More than that, it's what pushes me to carry on in all this. Because I often say to myself, "I've had it," but the study group stimulates me to carry on. If I were to evaluate all the things I do in one day—well, there's thousands of them. I may not get paid much for them, but they give me a lot in other ways. I very much value working in a group, with researchers, receiving what they have to offer; designing projects I want to do and having their support and guidance.

Perpetual Frustration: Alvaro Canales

I began my studies in the Universidad de Chile at the campus in the southern city of Talca in 1969. Three years later, when I was in my second year, I had to move to Santiago to live, for personal reasons and family problems. I carried on studying in the Pedagógico of the Universidad de Chile in Santiago, in the Department of Mathematics. I was twenty-three or twenty-four years old; I had got married the year before and hadn't completed the academic year, as my son died; afterward I took up my studies again in a normal fashion, until 1973. In 1972 I was in the third year and doing some fourth-year subjects as well.

During that year I saw an advertisement on the mural newspaper of the campus, offering work as a teacher, and it occurred to me that I might start teaching before I qualified. There were quite a lot of opportunities for teaching at that time, as all the qualified teachers were fully occupied. There was a need for people with a good level of training who could work. So I went along to a government school. They interviewed me, took my CV, and sent it to the ministry, which assigned me a steady job as a math teacher. In 1973 I was teaching in a high school and studying in the university still. Of course, I thought it would be quite difficult, studying and working at the same time, but I had a lot of responsibilities after so many family problems, so I just accepted the situation. I stayed up very late correcting exams, preparing classes, et cetera . . . and then it was 1973.

By September 11, 1973, I had participated in a series of activities that could be described as having a political nature. In actual fact I didn't really do anything in particular, but being active in the university during 1970 and 1971 made you want to get to know something of the slum areas, the precarious settlements, industries, because that's where you see what sort of social reality you're living in, and that's what made me participate actively, which meant being expelled from the university before I had finished my degree. There was a list, there were about sixty students on the list, and we were all thrown out for being political activists. With that sort of background, there was no chance of being able to continue to study in another university.

A Marked Man

All the universities were closed to us, all of them. However, they had given me a teaching post before 1973, and the school did not take any measures against me. But we knew that there was a list of about twenty-five teachers in the school, made up during the early days of the coup by the teachers that were in favor of the military action. They gave the list to the principal, and we were then like marked men, the ones who had participated.

After the coup, about three or four days went by and we didn't know what was going on. Nobody knew if we had to go to work or not. We were afraid to go because we didn't know if we would be detained—the politics of everyone in the school were no secret. I had been elected to a post in what was the Sindicato Único de Trabajadores de Educación about ten days before. So we were afraid, I was afraid. Finally, on about the fourth day I decided I had to go along and see what was happening. . . . There were documents that I had put away in a locker. . . . I thought to myself, if they look in the locker and find them and see my name, I don't know what might happen. These fears drove me to go to the school. I remember that I was a block away from the school when I met two or three colleagues who were in the same situation as myself. We looked around and saw nothing. We found the school janitor and asked him what had happened, and he said that some soldiers had come; he didn't know whether they had searched any lockers, but they had come and that's all he knew. "If you want, go in and look," he said, so we did and found that all the lockers had been forced open, all of them. Well, so we went to my house and discussed what to do . . . it wasn't easy. My father had been in the military; he was retired by that time, but since he had been a very upright man . . . he knew a lot of people. I had already spoken to him in case I had some kind of problem. By this time my brother was already in trouble. He was up north and had been detained up there. My father was very worried about him.

Fear

I was convinced I was going the same way as my brother; I couldn't sleep at night. It was terrible. My wife and I began to burn all our books. There had been a government publishing house called Quimantú, and we had books with no political content, but we were so afraid that we didn't even want them to find us with those books, so we burned them, at night so no one would realize. At that time we lived in a rented room, so we had to go out into the yard. Also, my wife tore books into shreds and flushed them down the toilet. We spent the whole night doing these things because we didn't really know what to do—I was conscious that at any moment . . . they could come looking for me.

After the day I went to the school, three or four more days passed, and then I got a telephone call at my mother's house from a colleague who had heard that there was to be a meeting at the school, and we had to go along. . . . That day, before I got to the school, I met some colleagues, and we started to tell each other that in this or that locker . . . and then—I'll never forget the moment—another colleague arrived who shared my political views and told us that he had gone to the school during the night and forced open all the lockers and taken out all the documents that might have been dangerous and burned the lot, everything. "So don't worry," he said. "You people haven't seen anything, you don't know anything, nothing, nothing." So we got to the meeting; I remember all the teachers were present . . . there was a captain saying he had been put in charge of education in that area of the city by the Ministerio de Educación, and . . . they treated all the teachers incredibly badly, all of them, without exception; the principal just sat there, but everyone else . . .

But finally I didn't have much trouble, nor did my colleagues. We just carried on working in the normal way. A new principal arrived in 1974. We had a very frank conversation with him and told him we had participated in the previous regime, but that we wanted to continue to work and as long as we weren't bothered, we would do a good job. There were twenty-four of us more or less. . . . He replied that if we worked loyally we would have no problems and could carry on working normally.

The following year, we got another new principal, and once again we had the problem of being the teachers with doubtful backgrounds. They started to take away some of the responsibilities we had. For example, I was the advisor to the Centro General de Padres y Apoderados; I was head of the Department of Mathematics and Physics of the school, without having qualified. But I have to say that the rest of the teachers were, let's say, older and hadn't received any training with modern equipment, and when we arrived we started to implement a more modern approach to math, with very good results. Many pupils got excellent marks, and the level in the school went up a lot, considering it was located in a comuna on the outskirts of town. The level was pretty good for that sort of low-class neighborhood. It was not just thanks to us but to all the teachers. Later on, the new principal took further measures; for example, he had glass windows put in the classroom doors, something that had never happened before.

I remember that he used to stand in front of the classroom door with a newspaper that he didn't read because, in fact, he was watching what was happening inside. What I used to do—because, well, it was pitiful to see him like that—I would open the door and invite him inside. I would say, "Principal, please come in and take a seat, you'll be more comfortable inside the classroom and be able to observe the class better." He had every right to do so, but I didn't like the way he did it. My pupils knew that I never entered the classroom if it wasn't clean, if the blackboard wasn't wiped clean, and if they weren't in their seats. I was very strict with the pupils in this respect and they knew why. Well, I was foolish that time, asking the principal in like that, and he didn't take long to start a campaign against me. Not long afterward he called me to his office and told me that I had acted in a reprehensible manner, that I shouldn't have behaved like that in front of the pupils, especially not toward himself, the principal of the establishment. I gave him my reasons. I told him that I didn't think his behavior was appropriate either, because he was the principal and had every right to come into the classroom. Of course, if he didn't want to come in, if he preferred to stand outside, that was his decision, but standing around outside did not look right to the other pupils that were passing by . . . and saw him there . . . it really wasn't a positive attitude.

Well, we carried on working with this principal, and I wasn't the only one to have problems with him; most of the other teachers did too. Usually if we arrived a minute or two late, we went to sign the register and found that he had already put an A beside our names, as if we were absent. We were required to work on Saturdays . . . and we had to do it. . . . Then they took the Department of Mathematics away from me.

The salaries remained unchanged, that is, independently of what you actually did in the school, your salary was the same. The salary was not particularly good, teaching salaries have never been particularly good . . . and the conditions my family and I lived in, my wife and two children, were bad. We started out renting a room and as we got on we moved into a house, but always, shall we say, in precarious conditions . . . so much so that my wife had to go out to work in 1974. By that time we had rented a house.

Then we started having big problems about who could take care of the girls. Prior to that we had always taken turns, my wife and I. Sometimes I didn't have to work in the mornings, on other days it was the afternoon that I had free, and then some days I worked all day. When I had a free afternoon I looked after the girls; they were three and four years old. On other occasions we left the girls with my mother-in-law. . . . I got a really big surprise when my wife started working. She got a job in a store. The owner liked the way she worked a lot and offered her a better job, in charge of the salesroom. At the end of the month her paycheck was between two and three times what I earned!

In terms of present-day values, I earned about 36,000 pesos then—that's the equivalent according to my calculations at least. She earned an equivalent of 68,000 pesos—70,000 more or less—it depended on sales. At present-day prices again, our rent at the time was about 15,000 pesos—between 12,000 and 15,000 pesos.

But Even So . . .

We lived with many economic problems. We couldn't even dress ourselves more or less well, that is, we had to make a series of adjustments. When it was only me working we had a series of difficulties. I even had to have help from my father with food. My father was retired from the armed forces. So, since my mother and my other brother were alright, he could help me economically. When my wife started to work our situation really got a lot better, until she started having problems with her boss, problems not connected with her work. She told me she wanted to change jobs and answered an advertisement in the newspaper for a job in the center of town. About two months after her interview there, they called her up and offered her a sales position, so she went to work there. It was a large, important store. Since she already had some experience, she got on quite well, as they give you a basic wage and a commission on top according to what you sell. She got on pretty well and still works there today.

Besieged

As regards me—well, I carried on in the high school. But in 1978 there began to be changes in the school authorities. For instance, they got rid of the deputy principal who knew the past of all the teachers with problems and had always defended us, saying that while we had indeed participated in the Unidad Popular regime he had never seen us do anything that could be considered as harmful to education or to other people. He was the person that had always defended us, in spite of the fact that he had not supported the Unidad Popular government himself. He had in mind that we were married men or something, I don't know why he did it. . . . They sent him to another school and we were left without our accustomed defender.

New inspectors started to appear, and they gave me the impression—an impression shared by some of my colleagues—that they had instructions to make life difficult for us so we would get fed up and resign. I remember that it was summer 1978, because we had just finished the school year, when we went for our salaries. They came and asked us to resign. . . . Some of the teachers signed [resignation papers] because they had had enough, others didn't until they received the notification from the ministry, and the rest of us—well, we just went on working, knowing that one day soon we were going to have to leave. They did it in an odd way. My exit from the school was not as a result of an indictment or an inquiry or anything like that. I think that the principal . . . in 1978 he made me general advisor of the pupils' center, which was a very conflictive post, because I . . . could mobilize the pupils perhaps; it seemed very odd to me at the time, as there were plenty other people that he was closer to. In 1979 he divided the center into two—a morning center and an afternoon center—and gave me the latter. I talked to him frequently; he would call us to his office. He seemed to think we would just leave, that we were fed up. Once he even gave me the impression that he would help me get a job in another school. I found that very strange and said to him, "Why do you want me to go and work in another school? I've been here for years, and not just my colleagues, but also the atmosphere, the pupils—they're all very familiar to me. One tries to help the pupils through from their first year to the fourth year. That's what I think my job is, and it can be done better when you know where you are. If I go off to a different environment, I don't think I would be as productive as I am here." I thought it was very strange that he should be making me these offers. On another occasion he told me that he wanted to bring in another mathematics teacher—a friend or the son of a friend. I spoke to a colleague about it. The principal found out and was very annoyed.

Apart from all this, I had a problem with a colleague who had substituted for me in a meeting of the pupils' center. What happened was that I arrived later at the meeting because I had a class to finish, and I found a whole program for the celebration of School Week written on the blackboard. I thought the suggestions were quite good and asked if the appointed committee had made them. The reply was that, no, the lady teacher had brought the whole program with her. I said that wasn't the way the center functioned, that the pupils had to make their own proposals and that we teachers were there to say whether or not they could be carried out. My female colleague got up and walked out. I later learned that she had gone to tell the principal, in tears, that I had made her look ridiculous. The principal called me in and told me off, saying I had no right to do such a thing. I said that I could repeat everything I had said in front of the pupils to him and that I really didn't think that I had said anything out of place, anything that could have hurt my colleague's feelings, and that if a colleague were to say those same things to me, I would not be in the least bit offended; on the contrary, I would probably have apologized in front of the pupils . . . anyway it wasn't worth all this drama; but the principal didn't see it my way.

It also happened that I had taken on some class hours in physics to complete my schedule—I had done a year of physics in the university. So, since I had done a bit of physics and was the only teacher with knowledge of both physics and mathematics, they gave me those six hours of physics. I remember that, for the first time ever, that year they sent another teacher to check what I did in physics. It had never happened before, never ever. I later tried to find out why a physics teacher from another school had been sent to check on what I was doing. This cast doubts on my competence, in physics at least. I was furious, but I carried on and set another exam, a physics exam, I remember, and the principal said that he had to look at it first. He objected to it on the grounds that I was asking too much of the pupils, that the level was too advanced and that I wasn't following the program. So I said he could set the exam that he wanted, but that I had set this exam because the pupils were capable of doing it. Well, they did the exam and the truth is that the results were all around six; the lowest mark was 5.2 [the highest mark in the Chilean school system is seven]. Then he suggested that I had helped the pupils. So I replied that I was annulling the exam and that he could go and set another exam, with another teacher, and that I would not be present. They did another exam, and the pupils got on just as well.

Finally the school year ended, January came, and with it the rumors of the municipalization of the school grew. The education corporation of the commune was to be formed in 1979, and we knew that the high school was going to pass over to the municipal corporation, and that the latter was going to fire all the unqualified teachers as one of its first measures. That is, all the teachers had to have graduated; since I was not qualified, I had to quickly find something else to do.

When Will It Be Our Turn?

There were so many rumors; there were rumors of all sorts, because every so often they got rid of somebody else; of the twenty-four teachers that had had problems, there were only six of us left. We kept asking ourselves when it was to be our turn.

When I got back to school in January (the vacations were divided into parts so I had to work until the twenty-fifth of January), it was the fourth of January, and I found very few teachers about. I had a friend with an administrative job; he's the only one of us who wasn't removed, we don't know why. Anyway, he called me over and told me that there was bad news, but that he didn't actually know what it was. The principal came over and said it was a question of my resignation. So I asked him the reason, and he just answered that they were carrying out some changes in the school and he needed my resignation. I told him he was wasting his time because I wasn't going to sign anything. He replied that he would have to take other measures. I told him to go ahead and do what he wanted, and left. I asked my friend Francisco if he had heard that the principal was going to ask for my resignation, and he answered that he hadn't known. I left the premises . . . and started to think, well, it's my turn now. At that moment my world began to crumble, because, although you know there's nothing to be done, well, a teacher is a teacher, he's not trained for anything else, and I was accustomed to—well, I just felt it was the end for me at that moment . . .

At that time I didn't know how to do anything else, I was so used to teaching. Back in Talca I had worked in education; I had been doing it for years; how was I to change direction? I couldn't even begin to think of something else. When the principal called me to his office again, he tried once more to get me to sign my resignation, but I wouldn't. So he said, "All right, take your vacation." But I thought, if I take my vacation before I'm supposed to, I'll give him the perfect excuse to fire me. So I decided that, no, I would continue to present myself at the school until the day I was supposed to go on vacation. This I did, but they didn't let me sign in; the person in charge of the book you have to sign put it away and wouldn't let me sign it. I went to Francisco, my friend, and asked him to give me a letter that stated that I had been coming in to work, witnessed by two people, which he did. Finally January 24 came around and I could go on vacation. I asked Francisco on which day the teachers who were going away on holiday were expected back at school, and he told me March 1. . . . That year I remember that my in-laws had rented a house at the beach and invited me along too. I accepted, but I just went there to shut myself up, and there I was, shut up for a month and a half—I didn't even want to go to the beach.

Loneliness

I felt that my world was collapsing on top of me, despite the fact my wife had a job; but for me personally, as an individual, it was like the amputation of a part of myself—I couldn't imagine myself doing anything else. I said to myself that perhaps it wasn't going to be so bad, that I could find some other teaching job, that perhaps it wasn't going to be so bad. Well, the first of March came around. . . . I briefly considered signing my resignation—I thought perhaps it would be better to resign than to be thrown out . . . but then I decided that, no, I haven't done anything to deserve the sack, no, I'm not going to do it.

There was one teacher, a woman, who helped me a lot, the only one, the only real friend who stood by me there. All my other colleagues, well, when they see someone in difficulties, well, they just watch out for themselves. One suddenly becomes transformed into a rather dangerous person; to talk to him might not be such a good idea . . . so I found myself isolated. . . . When I returned to work no one came near me, except to say something like "I'm really sorry," but nothing else. The only person who didn't behave in that way, who said, "Come on, where's the funeral? Don't be a fool, you're intelligent, you're capable, you can do this or you can do that," was María Isabel. She was a real friend and colleague with true dignity, so much so that she said that the day I had to leave the school, she would leave too, with me. So I did feel I had some support, moral support of course, from her. So I went along to the staff room and looked at the board where they put up everyone's schedule and saw that there was another teacher taking all the mathematics classes. . . . Every day I went in and just looked . . .

They made difficulties for me; for example, they held the first meeting of all the teachers with class hours in the school and didn't let me in. I had no classes, nothing, so they didn't let me enter the room. I was aware the whole time that if I failed to go to the school, they could just sack me using the rule book.

They paid me my vacations, and for this reason I didn't want to miss a single day. I carried on going into the school for several months in these conditions until I received a notification from the Ministerio de Educación that in my case they were applying four articles. I was deprived of the right to give classes in the public education system; that is, I could no longer get a job in the public sector. I couldn't continue to teach, I don't know. . . . I went to the ministry, I presented an appeal, I hired a lawyer, et cetera, but since it was all signed and sealed in the upper echelons, there wasn't much that the lawyer could do. It was a "resolution," and they come from the State Controller's Office [Contraloría].

There were four articles—I have them here somewhere but I can't remember which numbers they were. The first one was that my contract had expired; that is normal because, as I hadn't graduated, they could terminate my contract when they felt like it; I couldn't argue with that. The second one, I think, had something to do with some bureaucratic argument—at any rate it was also unobjectionable. But the third one cited an article issued by the Interior Ministry that prevented the person from ever occupying a public post again; that is, they were firing me because I was dangerous. In fact, that didn't worry me too much at the time; inside I felt completely destroyed anyway with all that had happened. I was going to do something else, anything else. . . . You're a marked man, I told myself; while this government continues, you'll never teach again.

In fact, I have given a few private lessons, I have worked in institutes in the morning or on Saturdays, I've taught in private schools. It hasn't been a question of income—I just want to teach, not with the idea of earning money. For instance, I give classes in the school my little girls are in; I give extra math classes without charging a cent, nothing.

Reconto

Well, 1980 was a year that I did very little. However, I had always liked electronics a lot and had some ability in that line. I had learned something of electronics simply out of curiosity. Actually, before I studied to be a mathematics teacher, I had finished a course as an industrial electrical technician. That course will never be given again, because they paid us to study. Of about two thousand candidates, they selected thirty for each course—there were two courses, sixty people. I was lucky enough to be selected, and they gave us all grants. The grant consisted of food, money for transportation, and apart from that they gave those that needed it another sum to buy the things we needed for the course, paper, pencils, and so forth. Every month they gave us the equivalent of about 25,000 pesos today. That was in 1966. That year I worked for a company. I was there until 1968 and then they were going to send me to another. But as by that time I had taken my Prueba de Aptitud Académica for university admission and had got a place, I decided to study and left the company. My goal was to carry on studying.

Well, in 1980, since I had this diploma in industrial electricity, it was fairly easy for me to learn electronics by reading books, notes, and things like that. I decided to take advantage of what I already knew and opened a radio and television repair workshop in a little town in the South, near Santiago. Why did I go there? I wanted to get away from Santiago, I even wanted to get away from my family. My relationship with my wife wasn't working because of my problems. She had always told me I shouldn't get involved in politics but should think of my children and not go off to meetings and such like . . . so she blamed me for all that had happened and said that I had brought it all on myself so it was up to me to find the solution, I don't know . . .

We never got over this, although our economic situation later improved . . . because the split between us went back a long way. At the present time our marriage is bankrupt, for the same reasons: she can't accept that I have principles, that I am who I am even though I'm not teaching anymore; she thinks that a man should think first and foremost of his children and his wife, nothing else. I don't feel that way, in fact I feel the opposite. I mean I have always been devoted to my children, but not to the extent of living isolated from the world; I can't just be concerned about my family—there are other things in the life of a human being.

At any rate, I set up my workshop in the little town and in fact did pretty well. But I found it wasn't really what I was looking for. . . . The number of clients gradually increased, but there came a time when doing the same thing every day wasn't what I wanted. I kept at it for about two years and then returned to Santiago. I say return, because I was living in the little town. I had chosen it because my friend Francisco, who I mentioned before, offered me his house, just like that, not something that many people would do. So I lived there in his house. He didn't charge me any rent, nothing, and apart from that he even found a place for my workshop. The whole thing was a good experience, because I got to know a lot of people. . . . It also helped me put my ideas in order; it was the treatment I needed to be able to think about what I wanted to do. Getting away from Santiago for a while and finding myself in a very small town where at eight o'clock at night there's nobody in the streets gave me the time to think and work out finally what I wanted to do. When I came back to Santiago I had thought things over, and in the same year, I'm not sure if it was 1981 or 1982, I took the PAA again and qualified for university entrance.

I went in like a brand-new student. I had acquaintances who had done the same as I did. In 1982 I started in the Universidad Técnica. I had my classes in the mornings sometimes, and other times in the afternoons. It was a problem, as I had to work as well as study. Well, I had various clients in Santiago and I fixed their TV sets . . . so I started to do more work of this sort in the evenings. It made a bit of money, not a lot, but at least . . .

The first year went by. For me it was easy because it was a repetition of things I already knew. During the same year, 1982, I had the opportunity of starting a business with some other people. After all this time I still hadn't collected my severance pay from the school. I had a right to severance pay because I had been presented with my resignation, that is, they had fired me. I had no idea of all this until an acquaintance in the Controller's Office told me. So I applied and eventually they paid me. I got the equivalent of what today would be about 80,000 or 100,000 pesos. Around this time I was talking to a friend one day who had also lost his job, and he suggested that we start a company. "We should sell something," he said, and went on to propose office supplies, which he reckoned would be an excellent idea. I thought about it and decided to go ahead. We also went to see a relative, a woman with quite a large house, and she too became a partner. She contributed her house, the telephone, and the rest, and we began to work.

Well, we went out looking for clients. I had no experience at all . . . I had no idea where to begin, I had never dreamed of selling anything in my life. I remember that one day I just went out with Roberto, my friend, to look for clients, and after a week of this we found we had sold quite a bit. We started off with things that you find on any office desk—that sort of thing. I had no idea what they were called; I had to be helped by the clients themselves, and the funniest thing was that they did help me. I never lied to them, and explained that it was the first time I had done anything like this. We widened our range of products, and, to the extent that I got practice in selling and more familiar with the products, I started doing the buying. I got very involved in the whole field of office supplies and also did the accounting for our company; since I knew mathematics I found it easy. I did something of everything—price lists, dealing with salesmen. Later I became the manager and directed the whole thing. We started to do so well that after about a year we had purchased a vehicle—in just a year, it was really wonderful!

This all happened during the boom period, in 1981, 1980–1981—the economic boom. We were mainly selling to military institutions, which were buying 2 million, 3 million pesos worth of goods at a time. We had contacts through our female partner, and also because, well, I was familiar with the armed forces. I had no difficulty in going in and saying something like, "I've come to offer you these articles; we can sell you everything from a paper clip to the stationery, whatever you want, even whisky . . . " So, we suddenly found that the business was going fantastically well . . . it was spectacular—I bought a car, something I would never have been able to do if I'd stayed in education . . . I had never had a car before, never. First I got a secondhand Volvo, then another used car, and finally a brand-new car—brand-new. I would never have been able to do that with my previous work, never.

Furthermore, my girls had absolutely everything they needed . . . things got somewhat better at home as a result; however, regarding the split in my marriage, my view is a very personal one: when both the man and the woman work there's no problem, but it just needs the man to begin to slacken, and the woman starts to complain. Now, if she earns more than he does, a series of problems follow. You get told, "You don't work hard enough," "you take it too easy," and even "go and get a job as a garbage man." Women don't take into account the fact that, well, you studied to enter a profession, and that human beings in general . . . perhaps if I lived in a different type of society, I wouldn't have had to lower myself to do some of the things I've done. Of course, necessity means you have to take whatever work there is. But you can at least start out looking for something that has something to do with what you know and not head straight for something completely different. So I've had problems with my wife about work; she'll say, "Why don't you go drive a taxi? You've got a licence." In actual fact I did do that, I even had to do that during the really difficult times, but I soon realized that I couldn't just go on being a taxi driver, it wasn't for me. You don't always find what you really want to do straight away.

At least the work I had in the company was an office job; I'm not saying it wasn't different, but the fact that I was managing the operation, a bit like I had with my pupils—I had to handle five or six salesmen as well as the suppliers. I had to deal with all these people, and that contact made me forget what I was involved in, and also the money I made was good so that at the time I forgot my objectives a little. The thing was that the business went very well, so well that I could buy all that stuff.

[Canales's economic well-being and his feelings of success ended abruptly when he and his partner Roberto realized that they had been swindled by their other partner, the female relative, who had put everything in her name and finally got the whole business to herself. When Alvaro realized what was going on, he started a rival business on his own.]

I had no partners, because Roberto went to Argentina. He had lost the same as I had, but he got together a bit of money—he had a car, like me—and went off to Argentina. Well, I started to work on my own, but I had to start selling cars, too, because we needed money to live on and money for the new business. The truth is that things really started to go well. I'm not a millionaire, I haven't got as much as we made before because the conditions are different, but at any rate, I make enough to live on and pay what has to be paid. I have allowed myself certain pleasures; I've got a car that I bought myself. The other vehicles had to be sold along with everything else. At present I still work with some military establishments; that's what I'm doing these days, I'm still in the same line of work.

Going back to the studies I had begun in the Universidad Técnica—well, in 1983 I got official recognition of the courses I had taken in Talca; that wasn't a problem. But the courses I had taken at the Pedagógico here, that's another matter. They are preventing me from finishing the degree course. I shouldn't have applied for recognition of those courses. It was my mistake. I applied for recognition for all the courses I had taken, both in Talca and in the Pedagógico, to see what would happen. If it worked and they accepted them, great; if not, bad luck. They asked me to bring a detailed account of the years I'd been in Talca and a certificate from the Pedagógico in Santiago. I had all my marks from the exams I had taken in Talca, so I took those along. Then I went to the Pedagógico and made the mistake of telling them why I wanted the certificate. . . . The secretary said that they would send it to the university for me, but they never sent the certificate that I had asked for, ever.

Maybe they sent something else, because I got called into the Department of Education at the university where they told me that the Universidad Técnica was to be changed into a private entity and called the Universidad de Santiago, and that the degree course that I was interested in lasted four years, and that my application had to be submitted to a commission. I said that as far as I was concerned I had no objection to having my application submitted to a commission. Then later, in my third semester, I got a call from the Universidad Técnica saying I had to pay an additional fee; otherwise they would throw me out—I've got the letter carefully put away here. At the time this fee was around 6,000 pesos and they were asking me for more than 12,000. I didn't have the money and didn't pay, so they threw me out. I've got all these papers carefully filed away. I think that there was more than money behind all this; I'm sure that aspects of my background had an effect. Otherwise it was quite a coincidence that so many things came together and prevented me from finishing my studies. After all, I wasn't a bad student, quite the opposite; I had no problems with the work and didn't cause any problems in the university—I didn't get caught in any sort of political activism, nothing, nothing. On the contrary, I was interested only in studying because what I really wanted was to finish my degree. All I did was study and work, study and work, study and work. And then they do this to me. I personally believe that it was all because of the report they sent from the Pedagógico when I asked for recognition of the courses I had finished there. I'm sure they still had the records where I was classified as a "problem student."

I began teaching back in Talca. I got the job through a fellow student who was in the fourth year at university and was teaching in Talca. He passed some classes to me . . . since I was president of the area of mathematics. At that time, the people from the provinces were a bit shy, and since I came from Santiago . . . I was always described as daring. In Talca the folk were quieter, they didn't rush about the whole time. There were fourth-year students, for instance, who didn't dare to give classes. This fellow student must have seen that I was different and asked me one day if I would dare to give classes because he wanted to hand the classes he had been giving to me—he was moving to Osorno. I said of course, why not? He told me that it wasn't complicated and sat down to explain the program to me, when suddenly up came the school principal. I was introduced, and the principal chatted to me and said he thought there was no problem because at the time there was a shortage of qualified teachers, especially in mathematics, so the school did accept math students as teachers. There I had my first teaching experience, thanks to acquaintances.

Before that I had even given classes in Santiago in an institute, one of the first to offer preuniversity courses because they had just started applying the PAA. They started in 1968, and since I had some experience with the test, we started to edit some facsimiles and to train people for the test. I worked only on Saturdays, once again thanks to a contact I had. A colleague—a fellow student really—also said that as I needed a bit of work he would take me to where he was working. What I mean is that I also got that job through a contact.

Housing

We started out living in my parents' house, and later we moved to my in-laws'. We weren't long in either place, not long at all. I didn't really get on with my mother-in-law, and my wife didn't get on with my family. So we decided to rent a room in the house of a Señora Silvia, who lived on her own near the Alameda in the western part of town. We lived there for nearly two years. The *señora* was a very nice person. Later she fell ill and her brothers took charge of the house, so we moved a block farther down. There we lived with a family for about a year.

Then we went to live in military quarters. An acquaintance rented us the house he had been assigned, very cheaply. Of course, you weren't supposed to do that, it was forbidden, and finally we had to leave. In fact we were quite ready to leave because . . . Living there was a shocking experience. The soldiers would go out on night operations and so on, and then next day the recruits would be sent out to sweep the streets of our quarter and sometimes they would strike up a conversation with you, maybe because you'd offer them some breakfast or something, and they'd start talking about all the frightful things they had done during the night. You just had to listen, although you hadn't actually asked any questions. So it was all a bit difficult, to put it mildly, and I decided we had to move as soon as possible. Then we had a very unpleasant experience and had to leave very quickly.

We moved to a sector of Parque O'Higgins, a rented room, with our two little girls. It was a tiny room; we'd had to leave so fast that we hadn't had time to find anything better. It was, however, near my family, and my mother lived in the neighborhood so we took the room though it was so small. I had to sleep over at my mother's house, and my wife stayed in the room with the girls. We paid the equivalent of about 5,000 or 6,000 pesos at present-day prices. I earned the equivalent of about 30,000, 35,000 pesos. We had the use of a kitchen—well, it was a sort of extra room, not really a kitchen. Although the house was very nice, we had problems and were only there about a month when at last we found a house not far away, in the same neighborhood. The rent was about 12,000 pesos at current prices.

This was when my wife started taking in sewing and dressmaking work. I didn't quite earn enough, and we also had problems with one of the girls, the elder of the two. She had to be in the hospital for quite a long time, and then it appeared she was developing asthma—it was terrible. The treatment was quite expensive; she had to be vaccinated on Mondays, Wednesdays, and Fridays. The money didn't stretch far enough to live comfortably; far from it, there were always money worries. Apart from this, I had other things to do as well as teach. I was obliged to use my knowledge of electronics, taking advantage of my diploma in industrial electricity. I repaired machines for waxing floors, washing machines, television sets. But I had very little time left over; I stayed working until very late in order to increase our income. That was when my wife started working, taking in sewing. After that the owner of the store employed her as a saleslady; then she had to leave after she had some problems with him, and moved to the job she still has today.

We lived there for about two years. We moved when the owner needed the house back and went to live in another house in the Avenida Matta neighborhood—a whole house to ourselves. By that time the girls were of school age, the medical treatment was finished, and my wife was in charge of the shop. So we had an easier time of it economically, much easier. We could even go out to eat sometimes, on the weekends we could take the girls for an outing somewhere, we could buy them things they asked for; we started to buy furniture, something we hadn't been able to do before, and we also began to save a bit, something else we had never been able to do. My income was tiny compared with that of my wife; she earned more than double what I earned. I used to get annoyed, as she had studied only as far as the third year of high school and then did the fourth year as an external student or something like that—anyway I used to add up the years I'd spent studying and say, "Why did I study for so long? To earn less than you do?" Well, that was when things got better economically. Our daughters couldn't have everything they wanted, of course, but we could give them Christmas presents, dresses, good-quality schoolbooks, pens, pencils, and so on.

We paid more or less the equivalent of 12,000 to 15,000 pesos for that house, but it was much better than the other one. The owner didn't seem particularly interested in making a lot of money with the rental; he was more concerned that the house be looked after properly. We found this house through my mother. She was sort of acquainted with the owner and that's how we came to be offered it. She spoke to this person and we took it.

After that—I was working in the high school still—we were always on the lookout for something better, and also I wanted to be near my relatives, in order to be more or less in contact with the family, so we moved again, nearer to my mother.

Relatives and Friends

A friend lived with us, a colleague from the school. He was separated from his wife, and so was a solitary fellow. Well, we would try to converse with him every day—because he was very withdrawn, you had to drag the words out of him. One day he admitted to me that he was truly in love with his wife, that it was also his fault that they had separated, because he had a very difficult character . . . and my wife, who would have made a wonderful social worker, took it upon herself to get in touch with Luciano's ex-wife and invited her to the house. There, naturally, she met Luciano, and they started to talk to each other and finally they got back together again and remarried— we were the witnesses of their second marriage to each other. Afterward they both lived with us for a while; we helped them a lot. Later they rented their own place and left.

He had also been fired from the high school, although he had thought they would never throw him out. They classified him as "available," a more elegant way of telling him to get out. Being available meant that if there was a class without a teacher he got it; if there wasn't he went home. That was the way they got rid of him. He got his severance pay and one day told me he wanted to go to Sweden. He had a friend in exile there who had written and said he was going to do the paperwork so that Luciano could go. So Luciano asked me what I thought about the idea, if I would go if I were like him—a difficult type who didn't adapt easily to other people. We got on alright, mind you. So he said, "If you go too, I'll go. We can stay there and maybe make a better life for ourselves." I spoke to my wife about it, and she said, "You can if you want to; otherwise you'll just brood about what might have been. You have to take the opportunities that life offers." So I said, "Well, that's fine. Let's go then." My work was unstable, the commercial part; sometimes the sales were good and sometimes they were bad—like any business—so I decided to go, or rather to try to go. We agreed, Luciano and I, that he would go first and then send for me. Well, off he went. We went to the airport to see him off, all very excited, saying, "We'll see you over there" and things like that. But we didn't hear a word from him for fifteen, twenty days, and then a letter arrived saying that he was fine and that he'd gone on a trip to various places, other countries; he'd been to Denmark . . . and he wrote in one of his letters—I'll always remember his very words—"Sweden is a golden cage." One day he just came home; nobody was expecting him, we didn't expect him—after thirty days he came back to Chile.

He had gone off on his own; his wife and children had stayed with us. When he came back with a face like . . . he was the same Luciano we had originally known, withdrawn, didn't want to talk to anybody. . . . "What's happened to you? Why that expression on your face? Did you have a bad time? Weren't you allowed to stay? Did you have problems?" . . . "No," he replied, "what happened was that my friend over there told me that the only way to stay is as a refugee like him, and I'm a coward. I knew I had arguments to present my case as a refugee but I was afraid that there would be reprisals against my wife, against you and your family. So I thought it over ten times, a hundred times, a thousand times, and finally opted to come back. That's why I didn't stay." "Well," I told him, "no one's reproaching you for not staying, on the contrary." "But the problem is," he said, "I've spent all the money I had, my savings, and now the future looks very black. What am I going to do?" We told him not to worry, that somehow we would get everything worked out alright. "You just went and then came back, so what?" Now he works as a teacher in a private academy.

My elder brother, the one that was detained up north, he was eight years without a job. He lived off—well, his wife is a teacher. Finally, given the difficult situation, he came down to Santiago. She stayed up there with their son, and he is living here with their elder daughter. They never really ever got on, he and his wife, but they never separated. He got the help that we, his family, could give him—my other brother, me, my mother—my mother luckily gets a pension, but she had serious difficulties because, apart from my brother, she was helping my sister, who was also living with her after separating from her husband, with four children.

My mother had a large number of dependents.... She's a good mother, she's always been concerned for us. In general, we brothers and sisters have always felt solidarity with each other so no one would get annoyed because Mother was helping my sister, or because my brother lived with her. On the contrary, we all tried to cooperate as much as we could to alleviate my brother's situation . . . until he could get a job. His problem was that he couldn't work in any sort of public institution; there's even a decree. He had the chance of going abroad, but he didn't want to, basically because of his family. He would have had to go with his daughter, leaving his son behind, and it appears that he felt that splitting up the family like that was not a good idea. He wanted to try to keep his family together at all costs—it was very important to him. He tried doing one thing and another until he found a job through a colleague.

My mother lives with him and his daughter at the moment, because my sister went to live in a house left to her by my other brother, who went abroad. He left it to her almost completely furnished. My sister manages because . . . she has an allowance from her husband, about 15,000 pesos, and apart from that, one of her children is working in a computing firm. . . . He's done quite well; he's a clever boy. He must be earning around 60,000 pesos at the moment, so he's the breadwinner—a sort of husband to my sister. I always tell her to look after him because he's a good kid, and naturally he also takes an interest in his brothers and sisters, in spite of the fact that he's the youngest of the family.

Another of her children had a job, but then had problems and isn't working at the moment. He's been about four months without work. The eldest was working too; he studied at night school, finished high school and . . . I would say he's a product of a bad period. He lacked the authority that a father provides, he got involved in drugs, then got treatment. I argued a lot with my sister as a result. Very recently he seems to have got himself together, but the whole business has left its mark and he's very shy. He's working with me now. . . . It's a help, and apart from the help . . . I'm frequently reminding him that you have to make an effort and get on in life. He wants to overcome his bad experiences, and the will to do so is essential. He's now twenty-six years old. He's an adult, although I tend to refer to him as a boy because . . . I pay him 9,000 pesos a month. It's not much, but he eats breakfast, lunch, and tea with me and we treat each other informally, as relatives; for me he isn't an employee, he's a member of my family. He is totally responsible for what he does, he can get home at the time he wants; I don't start making things difficult for him. Of course I am delighted to give him some responsibility, that's what counts. I have to try to guide him gently, and I know a bit about how to do that. You have to gradually make demands, otherwise he'll just get bored and leave. The idea is that in the long term—I'm sure he's going to change, he's a very orderly kid; that's of fundamental importance. . . . He just needs a bit more pushing, he needs a bit more strength, more interest in doing things, in life. He's still a bit down, well, very down, with no spark, but he's got good intentions; that is important. And I think to myself, if my brother could practically give a house to my sister, with a refrigerator, kitchen, dining room, library, I don't know, beds and bedding, I can help too.

Coming back to the story of our various homes; after the house near the Parque O'Higgins, we went to live in a very nice apartment, a really nice place it was, and we had the chance of staying there because the proprietor of the building, a factory owner, was a very nice person and rented us the apartment cheaply. I had been paying 18,000 pesos in rent, and when we moved to this apartment I paid only 12,000, and it was a far better place. The design of the apartment was better. It also had two bathrooms, maid's room, a very big kitchen, a big dining room, three bedrooms. It was worth a lot more . . . and it was well located. But soon after we moved in, the owner had problems. He bought some new machinery, and this was in 1981, 1982, 'round about, and he got caught by the fall in the peso and found himself with an enormous debt and went bankrupt. The company went bankrupt, and then he lost his property, his own house and then this building with about twelve apartments. One day we received notification that they were going to be auctioned off. He came to talk to us and suggested that we went to the bank to see if we couldn't get a loan to buy the apartment. Not just anybody would have bothered to come to see us. So we went along and had to make an offer. Everyone that lived there had to make an offer to the bank, but a large company made a bigger offer and bought the lot, even the street! We were disappointed because the apartment would have cost us at that time about 1 million pesos, and paying it off in twenty years—I think we could have managed. All the families in the building were more or less in a position to do it. . . . Well, it didn't work out, and the next thing was the new owners wanted us out fast. The old owner gave me a document saying we had lived there for ten years; he faked it in actual fact, but he said that there was no reason to make things easier for these people with so much money. He told us that we should get one month's stay for each year and so we could carry on in the apartment for almost another year, no problem.

I began to look for an apartment in the same neighborhood and found one through the newspaper, and that's where I'm living now. It's a few blocks from my mother's house. The apartment is not large . . . but it's comfortable, with four rooms, and there's four of us, so we're alright.

Now, we never bought a house for a very simple reason. Of course, my wife works in the big store and there they have a savings cooperative. They were saving up and the firm was going to contribute—my wife was very excited with all this. So much so that—the truth is that we had applied for a house through the Housing Service [Servicio de Viviendas] and they did offer us one, but it was miles away, very far out, and—I don't know, it's not that one looks down on these houses, but we're used to a different sort of environment; it's difficult to accept something less. One wants to improve if one can, but at least not to go down in category. They offered us a house in an area surrounded by slum settlements—the four streets they had built were surrounded by these settlements—and though the apartments were very nice . . . at present there are problems of delinquency out there. Well, after being assigned the apartment, I went along to see it. It wasn't bad, it had three bedrooms—it didn't have any finish on the floor, mind you . . . it hadn't been painted, a series of things that could have been fixed—but I said to myself, "If I buy this, I'll lose the opportunity of applying for something better in the future." Furthermore, I thought, my wife won't be able to take advantage of the cooperative, she might even lose the money. . . . She had found out that if I had a property, she couldn't apply for one from the cooperative, because they gave priority to the people without their own home.

Afterward something very odd happened with this cooperative business. They built some very pretty houses and signed an agreement with the construction company. By that time each member had between 60,000 and 70,000 pesos in the cooperative fund. Each person was to go to the construction company and . . . the money was just to pay the legal fees; apart from that you had to apply for two loans, one from the government bank [Banco del Estado] and the other from another bank. One loan, 150,000 pesos at the time, was to cover a part of what had to be paid directly to the construction company, and the other loan was to be paid in twenty years. I calculated how much this would be, and at the time it came out at about 14,600 pesos a month. We could pay that then, no problem, but they seemed to be in a great hurry for us to choose our house, which made me suspicious. I felt that there was something hidden, something that we didn't know about. So I spoke to my wife and said, "Look, I don't think I want to go ahead with this, I would prefer it if we got our money together ourselves, bit by bit. We can always just buy a piece of land somewhere we like and build a home in a place we like." The cooperative houses weren't ugly, that wasn't the problem, but there was something about the deal that put me right off. Well, we didn't go in. Several of my wife's work mates did, about twelve of them. They started living there, paying their 14,000 or so pesos. But then the monthly payments started to go up; later they were paying 17,000 pesos, and last year, for example, four of my wife's friends lost their homes because the monthly mortgage payments went up to thirty-something thousand, 38,000 pesos I think it was, and they just couldn't pay. They threw them out of their homes and didn't give them anything back, not a cent. Everything they had done to the houses, like putting up iron railings, new bathroom fixtures— they lost it all. One of them offered to transfer the debt to me so that we could have the house, but I would have had to pay up all the back payments and we didn't have the money at the time. The woman said to me, "It's a gift; I'd rather give it to you than the construction company." But we decided not to get involved, but to wait until we had the money to buy something outright.

I know of several similar cases; you start paying a mortgage—I'm talking about the middle class, not those little houses where you pay 0.8 unidades de fomento, or whatever it is, for a matchbox; I mean a house you can actually live in, with a garden, where you can live and you are not squashed into a tiny apartment—and the mortgage starts to go up and up until you can't pay it anymore. That's why we don't want to get involved in any of the possibilities they're offering at the moment. We would certainly qualify—that is, we've got a savings account—but I prefer to carry on paying rent. I negotiate with the owner each year, and we can get by alright. I don't think I'm the only one to think this way. My brothers also think the same. There's my brother that went abroad; I guess he'll be wanting his home here too.

Weighing Up the Experience

My younger bother is very tenacious; perhaps there's a difference between us in that sense. Suddenly I'll get a bit depressed—the business, for instance: I'll just feel like chucking it in. I shut myself away to think. There's not a real future for me in it. What I mean is, I'm doing it basically to survive. There are possibilities of branching out into other things . . . but they're just possibilities. Basically I live to pay the rent, to eat, to dress myself, and to give my daughters some of life's comforts, that's all. I could never say that I was satisfied, or that tomorrow I'm going to do something else—I'm going to open a bookshop in the center of town, or even have a goal like that—very difficult. . . .

Sometimes I walk past a school, or I have to go and give a class at my girls' school. At that moment I feel I'm doing something I really should be doing, because I am doing it with true pleasure; it's as if I become transformed. Then, when I have to go back to my current work, because I do it with a sense of duty and not pleasure, well . . . of course, I tell myself, there are pleasurable aspects; there are rewards too at times; there are moments when the business is going very well and I think that, well, it was worth it after all, and I'm encouraged to carry on. But when I look back at my life since I started the business, it feels like I've just been doing my duty, and when it comes down to it and I see the years going by . . . I am forty-three years old now and I feel the years passing inexorably. I feel that I'm on the downhill slope, that I haven't that much time left. As for the future, I don't know what awaits me. The business could go well but might not—it's uncertain, especially for someone like me with no economic backup. If I had 3 million pesos in the bank, for instance, 4 million pesos, I would be less concerned. I could work with that money and make it grow. However, right now I have very little put away and so . . . Now, when my brother left and told me that he might send for me later on, I start thinking that perhaps I'd be better going abroad for five years or so, maybe I'd make more.

I have to think of the family. My girls are about to start university. One of them is about to finish the fourth year of high school, and the possibilities that they have here with the system we've got, where education is very expensive . . . not the high school that my girls are in; there you pay the registration and the quota for the parents' center. In the municipal schools you pay the registration fee and the quota fixed by the Centro General de Padres y Apoderados. The latter is obligatory, but you can pay it in monthly instalments. It depends on the schools, where they are located—their socioeconomic environment. In some schools they charge 3,000 pesos, and in others 5,000, 6,000; it depends where the school is. But in general, elementary and high school education is free. Putting the girls in the school they're in was not easy. For a start they had to have a certain grade average, and then—and I say this quite seriously—they have to be the daughters of members of the armed forces in order to be accepted. This high school is full of people with connections in the armed forces, uniformed and plainclothes police. We managed it because I had some colleagues who were acquaintances there, and the secretary of the principal had worked in the same high school I had worked in, so that's how I got the girls accepted, over and above their good averages. I managed to speak to the secretary, and she had a word with the principal.

Being a Teacher

I was somewhat involved in professional organizations, in the Asociación Gremial de Educadores de Chile, the AGECH, when it was separate from the Colegio de Profesores. They broke into our headquarters several times.

I would really like to be involved in education at the present time. I've been to schools in Pudahuel, Conchalí, La Cisterna, and I have to admit that educational standards seem to be declining in a terrible manner. Why is this? For a start, the programs are full of holes; some even have errors. In particular there are problems with the way the different courses or subjects are divided up between science and humanities. It appears that the people that are currently doing this task are not very well trained for the job. I also think that education at the present is elitist; that is, if you've got money you can buy a better education. The people without money, in the slum settlements—San Gregorio, La Victoria, or wherever—are getting a minimum of education. Now why is this? First because the municipalities are paying the teachers the minimum. It depends on your seniority, but roughly speaking, the salaries in the municipalized schools oscillate between 30,000 and 50,000 pesos. In the schools in Providencia and on up into the neighboring areas, the study of two languages is obligatory for all pupils, but in all the schools on the outskirts of Santiago—if we were to go out and ask one day, we would find that they teach only one language.

Regarding the teachers, the salaries are better in the private schools—

they all earn around 100,000, 80,000 pesos. There aren't that many private schools so it's not easy to get that sort of job. If you go and apply for a job in a private school, they ask for all your background, you have to present a CV, and I think that to a large extent they also take a close look at your surname. I presented my CV at lots of private schools, but they never offered me a job. Contacts help, of course—that is, I've always said that this country is a country of friends.

You could say that I'm a person who has had friends. I've thought of them as friends. But I don't think of friendship as a sort of brotherhood that you have to keep demonstrating. For me, friendship is disinterested, it's something that you feel for another person, who may or may not reciprocate; it doesn't matter either way, because friendship is like that; you give but you don't necessarily receive anything in return. The case of Francisco, for instance—sometimes there are things that go beyond friendship, like in the case of Francisco. At the moment we don't see anything of each other, but if tomorrow we met up it would be as if we had never been apart. There's no reproach, bad feelings or anything like that. That is friendship for me; it's permanent. Naturally you give a lot, sometimes just trying to help solve problems. We've all got problems.

I think that teachers especially are living very much a life of appearances. In general, a teacher is very concerned with appearances. For example, we have to be well dressed, know how to present ourselves to the class, speak well, never show our weaknesses, although of course we all have them. Because behind each one of us is a drama, the family, the life-style that we have to try to achieve—is that not true? We have to fight for it. And as I have always said, the unfortunate thing about teachers is that all they know is how to teach. I was lucky enough to learn other skills, but most teachers don't know how to do anything else. Several colleagues of mine at the moment are out of work as teachers and are having to do something else that they don't enjoy because it's just not their work. . . . That's why they always say that we teachers are a bit quixotic. Despite the fact that I haven't actually graduated, I feel I am a teacher—a good teacher, what's more, with a very good training. I never had problems with my pupils regarding the quality of my teaching.

Just Life: Fernando Morales

I am a teacher of natural science and biology. I graduated from the Universidad Católica de Chile. My wife is Eugenia Jeria, from the Universidad de Chile, an elementary school teacher. We have two children, a boy of one year, one month, and a girl three years, four months old. . . . My wife and I work in a school run by the La Salle religious order; it's a high school. She works morning and afternoon, and I work part-time. I work twenty chronological hours there and, apart from my professional activities, teaching first to fourth grade of high school biology, I am also a salesman for a pension fund.

My wife earns approximately 78,000 pesos before tax for her two shifts; that's about 62,000 net. My gross salary from the school is around 40,000; that's 35,000 net more or less. Between the two of us we earn around 100,000 pesos as teachers. Now, I'll give you an idea of what our normal expenses are: we spend about 33,000 pesos a month on food; in rent we pay 20,000; and our other basics, like the telephone, electricity, and gas, account for about 10,000. That all adds up to 65,000 pesos. The maid gets 15,000, and then our daughter, Fernanda, goes to kindergarten, which is another 10,000 including transport and tuition. If there's anything left over—gasoline, the car.

What I earn from the pension fund is extra. I've been involved in this only for a couple of months. Before, I worked full-time as a teacher. Up till August I worked in two schools, the subsidized school I'm still in part-time and a government-run school. I earned about the same in the latter as in the former, let's say 40,000 pesos. I earned a total of about 80,000 altogether then. We were a little bit better off then. But the government school job was only a temporary one. The termination of the contract coincided with a serious problem: we had a car accident and got ourselves into debt to the tune of about 500,000 pesos, what with fixing the other car, paying some sort of indemnification to its owner, and then fixing our own car, et cetera. It was my fault entirely and, well, I assumed the responsibility straight away and had to pay up. In addition I still owe the Universidad Católica money because I was given a grant to study.

I left university in 1980 when I was twenty-four, and worked for about six years as a teacher, without graduating. To graduate you had to take a seminar course, and I still had a bit to finish. I finally finished in 1986, having gone over the limit of time allowed by the university regulations. Furthermore, I went all that time without getting my debt sorted out. I was teaching and also worked as a research assistant in the university itself.

Then—well, I had other plans; I got married and my expenses changed. Up till that moment my idea had been to continue my academic career in research, in biology. But as a research assistant I couldn't finance anything. So once we decided to get married, I had to improve our income; I had to take on more class hours and get my degree. [Before he could do so, however, Fernando had to clear his remaining debt from his government educational grant.] Since 1986 I've been paying between 10,000 and 15,000 pesos a month, with a few breaks, periods of two or three months when I didn't pay. There is a certain amount of flexibility when they see that you are paying something; I've made use of various extensions; now with my last IOU—I still owe about 140,000 pesos to be paid by the end of October—they let me give them a check dated six months ahead. I have to cover that check for the 140,000 pesos and then I've finished paying, finally. The problem is that the car accident coincided with all this and forced me for the first time to try my hand at selling, in this case, something as intangible as a pension.

The pension fund gives me a basic salary of 15,000 pesos, more or less, and then I have goals to achieve. So what I receive is variable; it depends on how I do each month. However, the contract requires that each month you sign up a number of people whose joint earnings add up to about 800,000 pesos in taxable income. For example, I could sign up four people with 200,000, or eight with 100,000. This gives me a commission of about 60,000 pesos. Last month, my first month in all this, I earned 72,000 pesos. I got involved in this work through a friend who also sells the same thing. She told me about it. They give you training courses, which were quite good, and a lot of support and promotional materials. I got a full week's training before starting out.

As a teacher . . . I went straight into the school I'm in now; we both did. We met in 1981; we started work in March—it was the first job for both of us, we were both newly out of university. We got married two years later, in the school itself. The principal married us. Even the wedding party was held in the school. I got the job there quite by chance. I was in the university choir. There were students from other degree courses in the choir, and somebody heard that I needed to find some teaching work and told me of a friend of his, a counselor in the school, who said they needed a biology teacher. I got in touch with the counselor, and after a couple of interviews they offered me a job. I've been there ever since. I never took on long hours there. I've been in other schools too, and I've also worked in Conchalí, which is a much poorer neighborhood.

Usually high school teachers have contracts for a given number of hours, not full-time contracts. So it's difficult to work just in one school and work full-time. It's really possible only in the big schools with lots of groups at each grade level, where they can offer you enough hours to complete a full day's work. At times I've worked in three different schools simultaneously. Now this La Salle school is the one that's paid me the best. The other schools I've worked in were also private subsidized schools. On average they pay about 900 pesos the class hour. Suppose you have fifteen class hours a week, they pay you fifteen hours, not fifteen multiplied by four which, would be the projection of the class hour. So, a person who works fifteen hours in a private subsidized school—we're talking about hours of teaching—receives a salary of about 15,000 pesos a month; a little less, an average of 14,000. In the school I'm in I do twenty hours of classes and earn 32,000 pesos, which is quite exceptional in the market of private subsidized schools.

Now, with two or more jobs, you have quite an expense in transportation. There have been times when I have been able to get from one place to another only by car; there was no other way. Up till August, when I still worked in the government school, there were days when I needed the car; otherwise I would never have got there in time. Having a car costs quite a bit. When we started our life together we were paying for our car, and at least half our monthly income went on the car payment. When we got married we got together about 50,000 pesos, and the monthly payments were almost 30,000.

[Eugenia tells us something of her story]: I finished my studies in the Universidad de Chile. Pedagogy had not yet been taken out of the university. The Metropolitana didn't exist, unlike today. I started to work in the La Salle school because my sister worked there. She told me they needed teachers. I went along and got a temporary job. That is, before I went in with Fernando, I did a temporary job there, from September to December more or less. The following year they gave me a contract to work mornings and afternoons straight away, and there I have stayed ever since.

My sister did not study in the Universidad de Chile. She left school after the fourth grade of high school. In those days you could teach without having qualified or when you were studying at a teacher-training college. They contacted my sister when they needed someone on a temporary basis. She accepted the work; in fact, she was on vacation at the time. Later on she studied in the Universidad Católica of Valparaíso, which had a campus here in Santiago, and graduated.

[Fernando takes up the tale of the Moraleses' life]: Nowadays you can't work as a teacher unless you've qualified, so all the people that started teaching before graduating—and there were a lot of them; up until a few years ago there were a lot of people teaching without having graduated—all went on to finish their studies and were given training courses, so now there ought not to be anybody teaching without a degree. Many teachers who hadn't graduated were fired two years ago; they were dismissed en masse—there was a sort of little earthquake in the profession. This was only a part of the problem, the lesser part. . . . There was a problem of rationalization. For example, I studied in a government-run school where it was established that every so many years the teachers moved up a level; it was all reflected in their earnings of course. You earned more according to your seniority, your training. There were quite a few auxiliary personnel, laboratory personnel, librarians, et cetera. When this school was transferred into municipal hands, the budget was drastically reduced. Now the state subsidy isn't enough to cover all those increments in income deriving from changes in level. Nowadays in a municipal school, teachers earn more or less the same whether they've two years' experience or twenty. There's far less difference than before. And the differences that there are depend on the particular municipal administration. Naturally this has affected the quality of education, without a shadow of a doubt. The state has decided to lower the educational level. Without any doubt, municipalization meant changing the system of classification and remuneration of personnel, which, in turn, has saved an extraordinary amount of money. You can now maintain a school of four thousand pupils with the same amount of money that a school of two thousand pupils cost before.

There are a lot of other factors. I don't know if the problem is so much a question of budget reduction or if it has more to do with an increase in the population of school age. There's something of this behind it all. The intention is a good one, if you look at it calmly. There was certainly a lot of attrition before, and pupils still often fail to finish the cycle they start. But today, for instance, the legal permitted number of pupils per class is forty-five. My wife works a morning and an afternoon shift with forty-five second-grade elementary school children of seven years old in each one. This is obviously too many. And quality must be affected—one teacher per group, with no assistants, nothing. This is what's happening. Today, for example, a municipal school would not spend money on a librarian, on a lab technician, an audiovisual technician. It wouldn't have the wherewithal for it.

I studied in a very prestigious government school from fourth grade primary to fourth grade of high school; that is, I was nine years there. The difference between that and a municipal school today is enormous. I am fortunate enough to be able to make the comparison, and the difference is stratospheric, like between heaven and earth. The specific differences between the teaching in schools that are now municipal but were government-run and the old government-run schools—well, there are a lot. First there's the number of pupils. As a teacher, I never experienced a group of more than thirty-five pupils, and our school attended to a large population; it was a school that worked with a full complement of pupils in every grade. Second, and I am referring to infrastructure, I remember in my subject, a scientific subject, I was never without an assistant for any practical or laboratory work with the pupils. I remember the assistant in my school very well; he was a trained teacher, he wasn't just anybody.

Everything they try to make out is very up-to-date nowadays, the latest innovation, I mean the extracurricular activities in support of the formative role of the school—I'm familiar with all that, since I entered a government-run school in about 1965. When I was in fourth grade of elementary school, extracurricular activities were as systematically organized and considered as important as the main activity of the school, the main academic activity. We had to belong to a club, for example. The same way that I had to attend my math class, I had to join a club or a workshop. I was in a series of different workshops. I ended up liking theater best, but I had been in chess, puppetry, plastic arts, whatever; the school had all this. Furthermore, the style was very different. Nowadays they've got what is called the person-centered program of study, according to Decree No. 300. These are new programs . . . that have been implemented only over the last four or five years. Basically they divide up the pupils at the end of middle school according to their areas of interest, their vocations and inclinations. They follow either sciences or humanities. This is treated as some sort of novelty. All my high school years in that government-run school we were assigned to a humanist, a scientist, a biologist, a mathematician. In my case in particular, I got a bit of everything. What I mean is that what is treated today as something new, I lived through in my own education years ago.

I must admit that my school was exceptional; it was an experimental school and probably had a bigger budget than other schools. But I remember other schools of the same type—El Aplicación, Instituto Nacional, Amunátegui, Liceo No. 1 for Girls, Gabriela Mistral. They all had similar characteristics as regards pupils, resources, and size. Today these schools are all municipal, they belong to the Municipality of Santiago. I have friends and acquaintances that teach in them, I know some of the inspectors, so I have a good idea of what's going on in these schools.

As regards salaries, the teachers are all very badly paid. Of course, there are teachers earning 250,000 pesos. For example, I know an exclusive, top-notch private school, with a very high academic standard—it has university teachers, that is, teaching full- or part-time in universities, people with postgraduate degrees; there's nobody there with less than a masters' in the area of education. They earn even more than a university teacher. I know some of the teachers, and they are earning more than 200,000 pesos. I don't know if there are schools paying more. It is the most extreme case that I know. I wouldn't be surprised if there were not something even more exclusive. But I don't know how far they might go where salaries are concerned.

However, the average earnings of an ordinary teacher working full-time, forty hours, is not more than 50,000 pesos, independent of seniority. It's difficult to maintain a home with an income like that. How do you survive? Well, you have to cut down on your expenses.

But I feel that I personally need to do at least a couple of further education courses now and again. My area is biology. What I teach this year is very different from what I will be teaching next year. Every time I have the chance of doing a course I am aware of this. I should subscribe to periodicals and magazines, I should attend at least two short, intensive courses a year in my area. These are my needs. I need to read at least one book a month—access and, above all, time. I think that even if I had the resources, I wouldn't have the time. When I say hours, I mean class hours;

that doesn't include a single minute of correcting work, preparing material, planning classes. All that takes me an enormous amount of time. I don't know if I'm very slow, but it takes me a lot of time. What has happened is that I have had to turn myself into a rather spontaneous teacher. I have the program in my head and I follow it and do the best I can, but I must admit that it's not the best way to go about things. I work on weekends. It takes me about three hours to design a good test with about twenty-five multiple choice items, a few true/false ones, and some short essay-type questions. And I should do one of these every two weeks—I say "should" because it's impossible of course. You should do one of these tests at the end of every learning unit. When I was in the government school, I did get near this ideal, as I had thirty hours then and only twenty were class hours; the other ten were precisely for this type of activity—a rather special situation.

Teaching as a Profession

I am in a difficult profession, badly paid, and furthermore, hard work. Since I belong to the middle class, I needed a loan to study and I'm still paying that off. My family is an ordinary middle-class one. My father is an accountant. He has an office of his own, and his clients. . . . I have seven brothers and sisters. By the way, none of the others is a teacher. I feel that in social terms my profession has meant stagnation; in economic terms too. . . . I think that if you choose to be a teacher, you should be aware of the implications. . . . I'm doing this [selling pensions] for the first time. I don't know how long I will do it. . . .

It's the people with the most ideas, the most questions, who get most involved in education that find most obstacles in the system and the greatest limitations. Most of the time the latter don't really exist, however; they're just in the mind. People are afraid. For example, there are things that you don't talk about in class. There's muddled thinking; in my view a sort of cheap populism is sometimes confused with doing a good job in the classroom, especially when pupils from poor families are concerned. I think that this is a mistake. What I mean is that if you want to help the pupil you have to get the best you can out of him according to his abilities, give him some sort of future in life, not just make him conform and certainly not make things artificially easy for him. For example, we have a set of rules for the evaluation of the pupils that is a disgrace. Without going into detail, it is enough to say that for a pupil to pass a course at the moment he needs an average of four. That's relative—it depends what four actually means. At any rate, he needs a four, or else he has to sit for a written exam. If he still doesn't manage to get a four, he can take an oral test, and if he *still* can't make it, he gets a special test.

And then there are teachers . . . of course, there are demanding teachers too; I know teachers who really work conscientiously but whose primary obstacle is the school principal. The teacher is pressed by the school authorities to make things easy for the pupils. I think there's something behind all this. The regime probably wants to improve, and thus be able to exhibit, school attendance and pupil performance. And how do they achieve this? Not by creating the social conditions that would allow a real increase in school attendance and improvement in pupil performance figures, but by making passing tests easy for the pupils, demanding a minimum level so that the pupils practically pass automatically from one year to the next. Thus no effort is required for a child to start in first grade and finish in eighth. That's why I say that this so-called child-centered education is very populist and quite wrong. They did do some evaluations, but then they suspended them three years ago, all of a sudden, without reaching any conclusions, without really analyzing the results. I think they realized what was happening, and since there are no published results, the whole subject is closed. I would guess that the results were dreadfully bad.

This questions the whole issue of municipalization. The regime is interested, it's the work of the regime and it need not have been a bad thing, because . . . In effect, if we say "municipal school," we could be talking about a community school, and in that case we would say "great," wouldn't we? Everyone is involved in the enterprise. But we would have to have an elected mayor, don't you think? Not one appointed from above. We would have to have elected neighborhood committees; the schools would be run by foundations or commissions—I don't know how to call them, but all the groups affected or involved would participate: the teachers; parents; I don't know, the appropriate technical organism.

But Life Goes On

This school we're in is really quite exceptional from the human point of view. This is one of the reasons that I would have difficulty leaving. I'm not talking about the school authorities. When faced with situations, emergencies that a teacher might have, they act like any other merchant. That is, they defend themselves and their things and that's that. We know that we can't expect much there. But between ourselves, as colleagues, the almost spontaneous reaction when someone has a misfortune is to immediately start a voluntary collection as a gift for the affected person. We've signed a list promising a contribution on many occasions. You contribute according to your possibilities, 1,000, 2,000, 500 pesos, or whatever; it depends what the problem is too. When we had the car accident we received 32,000 pesos, I think it was. We're talking about I don't know how many teachers, that's not our affair, but it was as if thirty teachers had contributed 1,000 pesos. We really appreciated it because 1,000 pesos is a lot to suddenly give away. We are very grateful for that spontaneous help. We have our organizations as well—a small welfare organization (I'm on the board) that gives some benefits. For instance, if someone has a baby, or falls ill, or a close relative dies, the organization gives special grants of 4,000 pesos. We also give loans, a maximum of 5,000. The quota is not high, so we can't lend more than that and pay for our cups of coffee at morning break. Most of the organization's funds go on those things.

In our case we can't count much on our families for help. Neither Eugenia nor myself has a family that suddenly has an extra 100,000 pesos. They would help us in an emergency, but we would have to pay the money back fast, at the most within the month. So we have had to take out a two-year loan from an institution.

Another serious problem in our everyday life is the question of the care of our daughters when we don't have a maid. . . . We have a neighbor who's also a teacher, but she's got her own problems. . . . Nobody can really help us on this—at the most for an afternoon, something like that.

[Eugenia adds]: of course, in an emergency I go to my mother. If she can't help, I try my mother-in-law. But my mother has the problem that she looks after her mother-in-law, who's an invalid, so to be worried about her mother-in-law and, on top of that, to have my girls as well is . . .

[Fernando resumes]: as for the neighbors—we've been here five years and we don't know their names. The neighbors have changed over the five years we've been here: those on the right changed once and so did those on the left. Quite by chance I do remember the name of the first neighbor on the left, but I've no idea what the new one's called, even though we have had to talk to each other on occasions; for instance, when his dog broke the wall dividing the two houses and we had to fix it up between us. There we had a totally circumstantial contact with each other, but no more than that. We didn't know the previous neighbors on the other side, nor do we know the current ones. We have no idea who they are; I don't even know how many people live there. . . . They've been here six months, more or less, but . . . we just greet them mechanically, that's all. In my opinion they are a bit withdrawn. One of the neighbors has a girl of the same age as Fernanda; Fernanda spends her time on her own and gets bored and complains, as she's doing now. Once I met the neighbor's wife outside. She was with her little girl and I was with Fernanda. I started talking to her straight away and said something like, "How nice to have another little girl of the same age next door, so they can play together, and so on, either in our house or in yours," as a way of getting some sort of relationship going. "That's fine," she replied, "it's a good idea," but that was that; nothing ever came of it. Once I said to her when I saw her and she seemed tired of being with her little girl, "Why don't you tell her to come over and play with Fernanda?" She agreed at first and then decided that better not since they were "waiting for Dad to come home." People like to appear to be able to solve their problems on their own; they have difficulty accepting that there are things that can be solved by joining forces with others.

We have made our friends through the family, or else they go back to our childhood. We get together with them. In my case my friends are from my childhood, mainly old school friends. We have some contact with people in the same position as ourselves, married couples of the same age, colleagues from the school, but we see them at the children's birthday parties, at that level, nothing more. Those are the contacts we have. Where finding a job is concerned . . . I have worked in six schools, in one of them permanently and for periods in the others. I found one of these jobs through an advertisement in the newspaper; all the rest were through personal contacts.

Now, when it's a question of an emergency, we have the family. But if it's a really serious problem, we have to resort to more formal institutions—loans of money, for example. If I can take out a loan and pay it off, make an effort and pay it off, I mean, well, I'll do that and avoid having to resort to the family. But if I had no possible way of paying off the loan, I would have to go to the family. If we were to have health problems, that would be quite a serious matter. There are hospitals that offer free health care for a certain type of person, for poor people. They are public hospitals. I'm not sure that the quality of treatment offered to the poor is very good, but on paper they are publicly run, and the treatment for the poor is free of charge; payment is on a voluntary basis.

I've been quite closely involved in solidarity campaigns, especially in the schools. There's a lot of this sort of thing in schools—at least there is in my school, given its pastoral orientation and connections with a religious order. A lot of emphasis is placed on values, on solidarity, and so forth. The regulations of the parents' center even specify that part of the funds have to be used for grants for pupils in that particular year. There are initiatives aimed at mutual aid; I'd say that there is a degree of sensitivity and commitment. But we all live with necessity, and one hears of some really dramatic cases. Sometimes you want to do more but you just can't. You can only help a little.

Well, apart from all my habitual activities that I have mentioned up to now, I also work at a night school, a private subsidized one for adults, for ten hours a week. It's a different level of teaching. I started back in July, mainly because I was curious. I had never worked at night, nor with adults, nor with such poor people. The school's in a sort of slum neighborhood . . . although the neighborhood is not as poor as some of the people that come to the school. Some come from other areas; not all the students are from the area the school's in. As I said, I had never worked with adults, nor at night; I was offered some hours of classes by a friend—that's the way it works—and it was curiosity that made me accept, as well as an interest in getting some experience in an area of my profession that I had never worked in. Later, with the car accident, I came to need the extra income—any extra income was very welcome. My daytime classes pay about 900, 1,000 pesos the hour in a subsidized school, while at the night school you only get 600 the hour, a lot less. So I earn 6,000, 7,000 pesos, because there is 1,000 more. I've got my debt payments programmed by loan. For two years I have to pay 8,500 a month on one of them. Then there is another bit that I have to pay over one year at 10,500 pesos a month. I also have a shorter-term loan, for five months, at 50,000 pesos a month. In other words, during these first five months, I have to pay up 70,000 pesos a month just in loan repayments. My big mistake was not having car insurance. I still haven't got [a policy], I can't afford it until I've paid the debts. Insurance is expensive—70,000 pesos a year at least. But I realize now that with the accident I would have amortized more or less five years of the premium.

Everything I earn from the pension fund goes toward paying off the loans. Fortunately I found this new activity that is letting me earn enough to pay my debts. . . . I would have sold the car if I hadn't got this pension fund job, or taken some other emergency measure. So we're trying to keep up our standard of living, and while I can sell the pension fund subscriptions, we'll be able to do it. These first five months are going to be the difficult ones; there are still four of them left to go.

Of course, even without the catastrophe with the car, we have always lived carefully. Everything has had to be calculated to the last penny—vacations, for example. Usually we go to Maitencillo where my in-laws have a house. If it weren't for that, we couldn't afford vacations; maybe a week somewhere. . . . There are other things: we are members of a Caja de Compensación. There are institutions that affiliate employers; these institutions finance subsidies for sick leave; the workers then have certain guarantees, benefits—for instance, near here they have a park with swimming pools, tennis courts, a casino, et cetera, quite well maintained in general and with a modest monthly quota; I pay 2,000 pesos and we have a free swimming pool all summer, tennis too. I like playing tennis, and you can play an hour a day all the year round. Recreation is important to me—at least a minimum, especially for the family. Recently we haven't been along to the park much, but the possibility is there at a low cost, thanks to these institutions. I suppose not everyone has access to something similar; it's just for the affiliated employees and it's not a universal thing. But most teachers have access to this sort of recreational center; it doesn't cost a lot, so I don't know.

7

Conclusions

The implementation of the neoliberal model, applied in Chile under political conditions deriving from the military government, affected three basic aspects of teachers' lives: their working conditions; their social resources; and the symbolic representation of their role in society.

Teachers moved from the public sector to the private sector in the sense that they became subject to the latter's labor laws, and at a time when legislation was becoming more stringent with labor. This placed teachers in a position where their previous job security virtually disappeared. They were suddenly obliged to negotiate their work contracts as individuals, following the law of the marketplace. The dismissal of large numbers of teachers meant that a veritable "reserve army" was created. Competition for jobs in the field of education was fierce, which pushed salaries down, forcing teachers to work double and sometimes triple time, without the opportunity for any sort of protest because the channels for the defense of the profession had been restricted. There was no more collective bargaining aimed at establishing salary scales and levels.

Apart from this, the growth of private education (subsidized private schools) was encouraged, which meant education as a business. In this sense, the administrators of education (be they of municipal or private subsidized schools) benefited from the extension of the working day (class hours) and the number of pupils in each grade. For the teachers this meant that it became impossible to prepare their classes and to improve, or at least maintain, the quality of their teaching. In this respect it is important to point out that further education courses for teachers all have to be paid for by the teacher, and few can afford them.

In addition, the reduction of government social expenditure basically affected the middle class, the class teachers belong to, because it focused on social groups in the most extreme poverty. The opportunities for health care, housing, and education for the middle classes and their children were all reduced.

Thus, the working conditions of the teachers suffered as a result of a lack of job stability; the possibility of arbitrary transfer from one school to another; the deterioration of salaries, with the loss of seniority and the triennial raises; the increase in the number of class hours and in the number of children in the classroom; and, finally, the absence of any defense by a professional association or union.

The loss of stability meant that compared with the past (independently of how precarious their economic situation had been previously) it became necessary to turn to very close and trusted family members, with whom there was a close relationship, for favors directly related to physical survival (housing, food, loans, etc.). This is more like the survival networks Lomnitz found among the marginal poor in Mexico, who faced chronic job insecurity and whose incomes derived from a system of social security based on their family and neighborhood networks. These exchange networks were necessarily small, given the limited resources of the members; for the same reason, the favors were used to deal with urgent and constant needs—small loans, food, accommodation, child care, information about jobs. We found this same type of favor in this study, and with reference to the same type of network—close family, close friends. Teachers find this situation disturbing, as our interviews showed. They were somewhat unwilling to talk about having to resort to this type of help and about the favors received, in view of their quality.

Previously, during the 1970s, while people also turned to family and friends in emergencies, the networks were wider; they were based on friendship and trust, an element that necessarily had to be present, even where family members were concerned. The favors were mainly of a bureaucratic nature. Briefly, in 1970 this social class had professional associations and unions to express their demands; they had access to political parties. Through these organizations, they had access to public administration as well. Whether the person was a public official, or the friend of a fellow member of the same political party, the fact is that he possessed resources that could be exchanged, and thus kept his exchange network active. And, at the same time, he could conserve his middle-class status through access to its symbols—bureaucratic employment, type of housing and education, and so on. None of the teachers we interviewed mentioned this type of contact or favor. However, we assume that this system of exchange still operated, but that it was another segment of the middle class that had access to it.

In the past, the use of these networks was considered to be normal; more than normal, it was perceived as the fruit of a positive ideology of altruism and solidarity. People spoke with pride of the favors that had been granted, associating them with positive qualities expressing friendship and generosity. A good friend was one who did you a favor, and who, when a favor was requested, did his best not to place the person doing the asking in an embarrassing situation. A person who was in a position to grant a favor but failed to do so was considered a "bad friend." In summary, the system was a reflection of class solidarity. This type of network was totally absent in our study of teachers.

The ideal situation is a society in which universalistic principles of support for all are held supreme, making such social networks for gaining access to government services unnecessary. When society falls short of this ideal, the individual resorts to his social networks, which represent the basic unit of solidarity in all societies. Life is faced collectively (family, friends, political parties) and not individually, alone; I have my group that will look after me, and I have to look to the best interests of my group. At the macrolevel, the welfare state (responsible, arbitrator, integrator) is the closest to this ideology of shared, collective responsibility. The changes introduced into Chile after 1973 did not just comprehend the implementation of an economic model, they also meant an ideological change as to the responsibilities of the state. Emphasis was put on personal responsibility, on individualism. This change is reflected to a certain extent in what the teachers say, and constitutes a second reason for avoiding talk about the need to ask for favors (a need that is imposed, despite the efforts teachers have made to triumph over the new situation they face in the labor market). They speak with today's values: "managing by yourself" is the important factor and a quality that confers merit or worth on the person; to admit the need for help makes them uncomfortable, since it detracts from their worth.

The effect of the economic model on teachers is seen with all its force when the schools are transferred to the municipalities, and the teacher comes to depend on the mayor, a sort of boss figure. The weakness of the teacher's position as a salaried worker is materialized in this relationship: he has to negotiate with this person and obey his instructions, even when they are inappropriate from the educational point of view; he realizes that he cannot show his discontent, as he may well lose his job. Thus, in addition to—and even as a consequence of—a deterioration in working conditions, there is the loss of the status of "teacher": when the ruling value is one expressing the sentiment that "you earn so much, so that's what you're worth," the feeling that the teacher's role is not much appreciated by society is reinforced. In the triangle formed by the administrator, the educator, and the pupil, the weakest side is the educator: the administrator runs the show as he pleases—there is no chance of appeal; the pupil provides the subsidy that the state pays on his behalf; the teacher, on the other hand, means expenditure and is expendable.

How all this affects teachers can be understood by remembering that they had always thought of themselves as part of a group of civil servants—servants of the state—responsible for the transmission of collective values, given the multitudes of children that passed through their hands. The new system questions this traditional role in that it removes the teacher from this group, turning him into an isolated individual in the marketplace, and atomizes the concept of education, varying the content and quality of courses as a function of the resources available in each concrete instance. Previously, curricula were unified according to ministerial guidelines, and the professional organizations had opportunities to participate in the formulation of educational policies. In all the years since the coup, throughout the succession of changes in educational policy, teachers have been excluded. As a result, the mystique or spiritual satisfaction of being a teacher has received a harsh blow, and teachers' self-esteem has suffered.

Our final conclusion is that, on balance, the outcome has been decisively negative in all the three aspects we have studied—living and working conditions, social resources, and symbolic role representation. Indeed, to further substantiate our view, we can point out that these losses were, in 1990, reflected in the demands made by the organization that represents the profession, the Colegio de Profesores.

We make through this study two contributions to our subject. First, we have verified the fact that one of the most representative sectors of the middle class in Chile has been severely affected by the adjustment policies resulting from the foreign debt crisis. This sector thus should be considered as one of the most important creditors of the social debt. Second, we have confirmed that, apart from measurable economic indicators, there are other variables that must be considered, those related to the theme of sociability and that fall within the scope of the symbolic—dignity, self-esteem, respect. These should also be taken into account when talking about the social debt.

Finally we feel that there is sufficient evidence to conclude that some segments of the middle class have suffered more than the working classes, whose position in the social fabric has not essentially been threatened.

Bibliography

Amalrick, A. *Will the Soviet Union Survive Until 1984?* New York: Harper and Row, 1970.
Arellano, José Pablo. "La situación social en Chile." *Notas Técnicas* (CIEPLAN, Santiago de Chile) 94 (1987).
Bahro, Rudolf. *The Alternative in Eastern Europe.* Oxford: Oxford University Press, 1978.
Bensman, Joseph, and Arthur J. Vidich. *The New American Society: The Revolution of the Middle Class.* Chicago: Quandrangle Books, 1971.
Blau, Peter. *Exchange and Power in Social Live.* New York: John Wiley and Sons, 1963.
Bohanan, Paul. *Social Anthropology.* New York: Holt, Reinhart and Winston, 1963.
Bottomore, T. B. *Elites and Society.* Harmondsworth, Eng.: Penguin, 1978.
Bourdieu, Pierre. *Le sens pratique.* Paris: Editions de Minuit, 1980.
Centro de Estudios Públicos (CED). "Estudio social y de opinión pública en la población de Santiago." Working Paper no. 83, 1987.
El Colegio de México. *Historia mínima de México.* Mexico City: El Colegio de México, 1980.
Correa Brito, Isabel M. "Evolución de los empleos públicos 1970–1986." Mimeographed working paper. Santiago de Chile: Secretaría Nacional del Empleo, 19.
Dahrendorf, Ralf. *Classes and Class Conflict in Industrial Society.* Stanford, CA: Stanford University Press, 1959.
Djilas, M. *The New Class: An Analysis of the Communist System.* New York: Praeger, 1957.
Flaño, Nicolas. "El neoliberalismo en Chile y sus resultados." *Notas Técnicas* (CIEPLAN, Santiago de Chile) 101 (1987).
García, Alvaro, and Andras Uthoff. "Aspectos distributivos de la política económica en Chile: La necesidad de pagar la deuda social." Santiago de Chile: PREALC, 1988.
García, Norberto. "Reestructuración productiva y mercado." Mimeographed working paper. Santiago de Chile: PREALC, 1988.
Giddens. *The Class Structure of the Advanced Societies.* London: Hutchinson, 1973.
Gouldner, Alvin W. *The Future of Intellectuals and the Rise of the New Class.* New York: Continuum, 1979.
Graciarena, J. "Las ciencias sociales, la crítica intelectual y el estado tecnocrático. Una discusión del caso latinoamericano." In *Las ciencias sociales en América Latina,* ed. G. Boils Morales and A. Murga Frassinetti. Mexico City: Universidad Nacional Autónoma de México, 1979.

———. *Poder y clases sociales en el desarrollo de América Latina.* Buenos Aires: Paidos, 1976.
Gramsci, A. *Prison Notebooks.* New York: International Publishers, 1980.
Historia de las profesiones en México. Mexico City: El Gusano de Luz, 1982.
Hoselitz, Bert. "El desarrollo económico de América Latina." *Desarrollo Económico* (October–December 1962).
Johnson, J. *Political Change in Latin America: The Emergence of the Middle Sectors.* Stanford, CA: Stanford University Press, 1958.
Kaplan, Marcos. *Estado y desarrollo en América Latina.* Cuadernos de la Casa Chata no. 37. Mexico City: Casa Chata, 1980.
Kolajowski, Leslek. "Filosofía marxista y realidad nacional. *Vuelta* 50 (1981): 4–10.
Konrad, G., and I. Szelenyi. *The Intellectual on the Road to Class Power.* New York: Harcourt Brace Jovanovich, 1979.
Lomnitz, Larissa. "Carreras de vida en la UNAM." *Plural* 54 (1976): 18–22.
———. *Como sobreviven los marginados.* Mexico City: Siglo XXI, 1975.
———. "El compadrazgo. Reciprocidad de favores en la clase media urbana de Chile." *Estudios Sociales Centroamericanos* 7, no. 1 (1978): 35–53.
———."Informal Exchange Networks in Formal Systems: A Theoretical Model with Special Emphasis on the Soviet Union's Informal Economy." *American Anthropologist* 90, no. 1 (1988): 42–55.
———. "Reciprocity of Favors in the Chilean Middle Class." In *Studies in Economic Anthropology,* ed. G. Dalton. American Anthropological Association Monograph Series no. 7. Washington, DC, 1971.
———. "Las relaciones horizontales y verticales en la estructura social urbana de México." In *La heterodoxia recuperada. En torno a Ángel Palerm,* ed. S. Glantz. Mexico City: Fondo de Cultura Económica, 1987.
———, N. and M. Pérez-Lizaur. *A Mexican Elite Family, 1820–1980.* Princeton, NJ: Princeton University Press, 1987.
Lomnitz Adler, Claudio. "Cultural Relations in Regional Spaces." Ph.D. diss., Department of Anthropology, Stanford University, Stanford, CA, 1987.
Marx, K. *El dieciocho brumario de Luis Bonaparte.* Barcelona: Editorial Ariel, 1968.
Mills, C. Wright. *White Collar: The American Middle Classes.* New York: Oxford University Press, 1951.
Montero, Enrique. *Traspaso de servicios públicos a las municipalidades.* Santiago de Chile: Ministerio de Hacienda, 1980.
Moreno, Roberto. "La ciencia de la ilustración mexicana," In *Anuario de estudios Americanos,* vol. 32. Sevilla, Spain: Escuela de Estudios Hispanoamericanos, 1975.
Navarro, Ivan. *Diagnóstico de la realidad educational chilena.* Santiago de Chile: Corporación de Promoción Universitaria, 1987.
O'Donnell, Guillermo. *Modernización y Autoritarismo.* Buenos Aires: Paidos, 1972.
Papaioannou, Kostes. "Lenin, la Revolución y el estado." *Plural* 41 (1975): 6–16.
Polanyi, K., Conrad Arensberg, and Harry W. Pearson, eds. *Trade and Market in the Early Empires.* New York: Free Press, 1957.
Poulantzas, Nicos. *Las clases sociales en el capitalismo actual.* Mexico City: Siglo XXI, 1980.
Programa Interdisciplinario de Investigaciones en Educación (PIIE). *Las transformaciones educacionales bajo el régimen militar.* Santiago de Chile: Publicaciones PIIE, vol. 1, 1984.
Ratinoff. "Los nuevos grupos urbanos: las classes medias." Mimeographed

postgraduate reading material. Santiago de Chile, Departamento de Sociología, Universidad de Chile, 1966.

Riveros, Luis Alfredo. "Distribución del ingreso, empleo y política social en Chile." Working Paper no. 25. Santiago de Chile: CEP, 1984.

Rodríguez Rossi, Jorge. "La distribución del ingreso y el gasto social en Chile." Working Paper. Santiago de Chile: ILADES, 1983.

Sahlins, Marshal D. "On the Sociology of Primitive Exchange." In *The Relevance of Models for Social Anthropology,* ed. Michael Banton. Tavistock Publications, 1965.

Schkolnik, Mariana, and Berta Teitelboim. "Encuesta de empleo en el Gran Santiago: empleo informal, desempleo y pobreza." Working Paper no. 6. Santiago de Chile: Programa de Economía del Trabajo (PET), 1988.

Stevens, Evelyn P. "Mexico's PRI: The Institutionalization of Corporativism?" In *Authoritarianism and Corporatism in Latin America,* ed. J. Malloy. Pittsburgh, PA: Pittsburgh University Press, 1977.

Sunkel, Osvaldo. "Perspectivas demográficas y crisis de desarrollo. Mimeographed. Santiago de Chile, 1988.

Téllez Girón, Alfredo. "Iniciación del brote de fiebre aftosa en México e investigaciones llevadas a cabo durante los años de 1946 y 1952." *Revista Veterinaria* 9, no. 1 (1978): 31–37.

Tironi, Eugenio. "La clase construída I. Apuntes acerca de la producción simbólica de la clase media." Working Paper no. 53.: SUR, 1985.

———. *Los silencios de la revolución.* Santiago de Chile: Editorial Puerta Abierta, 1988.

Touraine, Alain. "Las clases sociales." In *Las clases sociales en América Latina.* Mexico City: Instituto de Investigaciones Sociales, UNAM/Siglo XXI, 1973.

———. *The Post-Industrial Society: Tomorrow's Social History: Classes, Conflicts and Culture in the Programmed Society,* New York, Random House, 1973.

Warner, W. Lloyd, and Paul S. Hunt. *The Social Life of a Modern Community.* Yankee City Series vol. 1. New Haven, CT: Yale University Press, 1941.

Weber, Max. *Economía y sociedad.* Mexico City: Fondo de Cultura Económica, 1980.

Wright, Eric. *Class, Crisis and the State.* London: Verso, 1978.

Index

Academia Superior de Ciencias Pedagogicas, 40
Academic Aptitude Test. *See* Prueba Aptitud Académica
Access, 22, 25, 55
Administration: of education, 41–43; public, 30–31, 34, 66
AFP. *See* Retirement Fund Administration
AGECH. *See* Asociación Gremial de Educadores de Chile
Aid: mutual, 143–144
Alessandri, Arturo, 17
Amunátegui, 141
Arrests, 51–52
Asociación Gremial de Educadores de Chile (AGECH), 37, 135
Associations: teachers', 34, 35, 37, 81–82, 135; welfare, 143–144

Bahro, Rudolf, 13
Bankruptcies, 5
Banks, 17, 68
Barros, Juana, 56, 65, 68, 71
Bensman, Joseph, 10: *The New American Society,* 11
Berríos, Graciela, 49, 59; in private schools, 50–51, 58; on teaching, 69–70
Bribery, 30
Briones, Félix, 57, 59, 73; budgeting, 77–80; on education, 70–71; employment of, 60–61, 74–77; family of, 62, 73–74; networks of, 64–65, 68; schedule of, 82–83; on teachers' organizations, 81–82; on teaching, 72, 84

Budgets: personal, 79–80, 146; school, 139–140
Business, 11; establishment of, 124–126

Caja de Compensación, 146
Caja de Empleados Públicos, 77
Cámara de Construcción, 76
Cámara de Diputados, 40
Canales, Alvaro, 56, 69, 72, 73; attitude of, 134–135; business of, 124–126; dismissal of, 121–123; economic situation of, 123–124; education of, 126–127; family of, 118–119, 130–132; friends of, 129–130; housing situation of, 127–129, 132–134; impacts of coup on, 115–118; networks of, 64, 66; work environment of, 116–118, 119–120
Capital: accumulation of, 3, 13; middle class, 16–17; social and cultural, 18, 66
Capitalism, 13
Carrera Docente, 37, 53, 60
Cátedras, 35, 77
Catholics, 18
Centers of Parents and Guardians. *See* Centros de Padres y Apoderados
Centro General de Padres y Apoderados, 39, 117, 135
Cerda, Pedro Aguirre, 66
Chicago School, 2
Children, 83, 95, 101–102, 110; care for, 67–68, 79–80, 91–93, 111–112
Christian Democrats, 30–31, 66
Clients: political, 29–30

CODECO. *See* Consejo de Desarrollo Comunal
Código del Trabajo, 39
Colegio de Profesores, 33, 37, 59, 60, 69, 103, 150; demands of, 81, 82; elections to, 45–46
Collective biography, 49, 55–56
Colleges, 38, 63, 65. *See also* Universities
Comando de Institutos Militares, 36
Commercial sector, 3, 15
Communism, 13
Community Development Council. *See* Consejo de Desarrollo Comunal
Compadrazgo, 21, 22, 27, 30; favors in, 28–29; as network, 24–26
Competition, 26, 46
Comunas, 103, 113
Concentration camps, 52
Conchalí, 75–76, 138
Concursos, 77
Consejo Comunal, 42
Consejo de Desarrollo Communal (CODECO), 42
Consejo de establecimientos, 41
Consejos de Desarrollo Regional, 42
Conservative Party, 18
Consumption, 4, 5
Contracts, 138
Coup: impacts of, 50, 66, 74, 96–98, 115–118
Curricula, 39, 149–150

Dahrendorf, Ralf, 9, 10, 12
Debts, 63, 102, 109, 146; social, 1, 2
Decentralization, 41, 43, 44
Decreto-Ley No. 6, 36
Decreto-Ley No. 353, 39
Decreto-Ley No. 1289, 42
Democratic Education Workshops. *See* Talleres de Educación Democrátic
Department of Counseling, 98
Dependent relationships, 15
Detention, 36, 52, 96
DFL No. 1, 39–40
DFL 1–3063, 43
DINA. *See* Dirección Nacional de Inteligencia
Dirección Nacional de Inteligencia (DINA), 52
Directiva Presidencial sobre Educación Nacional, 37–38
Dismissals: of teachers, 36, 50, 51, 100–101, 122–123
Dijilas, Milovan, 12–13

Economy, 2–3, 5, 15, 113, 123, 149; and business, 125–126; and child care, 79–80; domestic, 78–81; and families, 111–112
Education, 3, 4, 5, 6 (table), 22, 33, 34, 35, 60, 63, 94, 107, 135; costs of, 58, 110; and income, 77–78; levels of, 70–71; and military government, 36–40; modernization of, 37–38; municipalization of, 41–43, 61–62; privatization of, 38–39, 147; public, 14, 17; state's role in, 43–44; of teachers, 74, 87, 88–89, 96–97, 126–127, 141–142
Educators. *See* Teachers
El Aplicación, 141
Elections, 82; in Colegio de Profesores, 33, 45–46
Elementary schools, 38, 41, 140–141
Elites, 13, 14, 34
Emergencies: assistance in, 80–81, 144, 145
Employment, 22, 59, 107; access to, 64–65; of Alvaro Canales, 115–118, 124–126, 127; of Félix Briones, 60–61, 74–77; of Fernando Morales, 49, 137–142, 145–146; public sector, 1, 5, 6–7; before qualification, 56–57, 58; of Sonia Salas, 87, 97, 98–101; of teachers, 34–35, 63; of Marcia Vidal, 60, 108–109
Empresa de Transportes Colectivos del Estado (ETC), 94
Escuela de Artes Aplicadas, 87
Escuela de Carabineros, 57, 74
Escuela Normal, 56, 57, 73, 74
Establishments council. *See Consejo de establecimientos*
Estatuto Administrativo, 34
ETC. *See* Empresa de Transportes Colectivos del Estado
Examinations: of teachers, 34–35; at Universidad Católica, 113–114
Exchange: informal, 25; market, 27, 29, 30
Executions, 36

Families, 27, 62, 109; assistance from, 64, 80, 91, 92, 99–100, 102, 103–104, 110, 127, 144; economics of,

111–112; employment of, 107–108, 118–119, 128–129; interactions in, 93–95, 130–132; as networks, 65, 67, 68, 148; of teachers, 55, 56, 73–74, 85–90
Favors, 18, 23, 68; bureaucratic, 22, 25, 65; in compadrazgo, 28–29; requesting, 66–67
Fees: municipal school, 135
Finances: educational, 42, 110
Firings. *See* Dismissals
Free enterprise, 18
Frei, Eduardo, 66
Friendship, 24, 81, 122, 129–130; ideology of, 26–27; as network, 64–65, 103, 104–105, 136, 144–145; and reciprocity, 25, 31
Further Studies Institute. *See* Instituto de Perfeccionamiento del PIIE

Gabriela Mistral, 141
GDP. *See* Gross domestic product
Gifts, 23
Gómez, Irma, 55, 56, 59, 64, 65
Gouldner, Alvin, 12
Graciarena, J., 15
Gramsci, Antonio, 9, 10
Gran Santiago, 5, 6, 36
Grants, 58
Guzmán, Pedro, 59

Health care, 4, 93; access to, 63, 94; for children, 67–68, 91–92; costs of, 78–79
High schools, 1, 38, 50, 98–99
Housing, 3, 4; cooperative, 133–134; economics of, 127–129, 132; for teachers, 86, 89–90
Housing Service. *See* Servicio de Viviendas
Hunt, Paul S.: *The Social Life of a Modern Community*, 9, 10–11

Ibáñez, Carlos, 22
Ideology, 17, 148
Immigrants, 18
Income, 2, 15, 77–78; extra, 145–146; improving, 137–138; loss of, 51, 118; teachers, 62, 63, 90
Individualism, 18
Industrialization, 12–13, 14
Industry, 15
Instituto de Perfeccionamiento del PIIE, 70
Instituto Nacional, 141
Instituto Pedagógico de la Facultad de Filosoffa y Educación, 33, 40, 50
Intellectuals, 10, 12
Investment, 2, 3, 4

Jeria, Eugenia, 137, 139
Jeria, Silvia, 65
Jobs, 14, 22, 88; creation of, 2, 3; stability of, 11, 50, 63–64, 147–148. *See also* Employment
Johnson, L. J., 14

Konrad, G., 12

Labor, 2, 10
Labor Code. *See* Codigo del Trabajo
La Florida, 95, 96
La Salle school, 139, 141
Latin America, 13; middle class in, 14–16
Laws: labor, 4, 147
Liceo No. 1 for Girls, 141
Living standards, 45, 110–111, 136
Loans, 4, 58, 68; emergency, 80, 144; government, 109–110

Macul, 86, 89–90
Maipú, 76–77
Maldonado, Ernesto, 49, 57, 71; after dismissal, 52–53; and special school, 53–54
Manufacturers, 17
Market, 2, 3, 4
Marx, Karl: on social class, 9, 11, 12
Marxism, 36
Middle class: Chilean, 16–19; definition of, 9–14; in Latin America, 14–16
Middle sectors, 14
Military government, 3, 18, 31, 66; changes by, 36–41
Mills, C. Wright, 9–10, 11
Mining industry, 17
Ministerio de Educación, 34–35, 36, 37, 49–50; employment by, 51, 62–63
Modernization, 1–2, 3, 13, 31
Money: in emergencies, 80–81, 145; networks for, 68, 105
Morales, Fernando, 58, 61, 73; friends of, 144–145; on mutual aid, 143–144; occupational history of, 59, 64, 137–142, 145–146; on teaching, 71,

142–143
Municipality of Santiago, 141
Municipalization: impacts of, 41–43, 61–62, 63, 77, 98–99, 120, 135, 139–140, 141, 143

Narbona, Ignacio, 49, 50, 51–52, 56
Nationalism: economic, 15
Navarro, Ivan, 69
Neighborhoods, 94, 144, 148
Neoliberalism, 1, 2–3, 4
Networks, 21, 22, 36, 68–69; and favors, 66–67; friendship, 104–105, 136; members of, 24–26; social, 64–66, 148, 149; teachers', 18–19
Neves, Tancredo, 2
New American Society, The (Bensman and Vidich), 11
New Businessman Plan. *See* Plan del Nuevo Empresario
Nueva Ley Organica de Municipios y Administracion Comunal. *See* Decreto-Ley 1289
Nuñoa, 107

Organizations. *See* Associations

PAA. *See* Prueba de Aptitud Académica
Parochial schools, 76
Parque O'Higgins, 128, 132
Patron-client relationships, 15
Peña, Carlos, 66
Pensions, 61, 137
PER. *See* Pupil Performance Test
Peralta, Santiago, 55, 56, 62, 68; family of, 65, 67; training of, 56–57
Pinochet, Augusto, 37
Plan del Nuevo Empresario, 7
Plan Laboral, 61
Police Academy. *See* Escuela de Carabineros
Political parties, 29–40, 66
Politics, 4, 22; activism in, 115, 116; teachers in, 34, 66
Poor sector, 2, 135
Poulantzas, Nico, 9, 10
Power, 9, 12
Prices: liberalization of, 3
Principals, 61, 117–118, 121
Private sector, 3, 14, 34, 77; education in, 22, 147; employment in, 18, 31; establishment of, 53–54; schools in, 40, 50–51, 56, 59, 60, 76, 135–136, 145

Privatization, 18, 38–39
Production, 12, 13
Programa de Evaluación del Rendimiento, 44
Program for Evaluating Educational Results. *See* Programa de Evaluación del Rendimiento
Property, 11, 12, 15
Providencia, 135
Prueba de Aptitud Académica (PAA), 69, 74, 113, 123, 124
Public Employees Fund. *See* Caja de Empleados Publicos
Public sector, 1, 2, 3, 4, 22, 31, 37, 50, 77; employment in, 5, 6–7, 14, 17, 31; schools in, 63, 88
Pupil Performance Test (PER), 113
Purchasing power, 2, 4–5

Radical Party, 17, 29, 30, 66, 88
"Rational-technical" system, 12
Reciprocity, 18, 21, 25; opinions about, 105–106; rules of, 23–24; types of, 27–29
Recreation, 146
Redistribution, 3, 27, 29, 30
Regional Development Councils. *See* Consejos de Desarrollo Regional
Relatives, 28, 31, 64. *See also* Families
Relief systems, 80
Resignations: forced, 119, 121–122
Retirement, 77
Retirement Fund Administration (AFP), 77
Rewards, 25
Rural sector, 2, 41–42

Sahlins, Marshal, 27
Salaries, 15, 40, 77, 78, 109, 118, 119; demands for, 81–82; public sector, 5–6; of teachers, 38 (table), 135–136, 137, 141; variability in, 138–139
Salas, Sonia, 56, 59, 73; education of, 88–89, 90–91; family of, 64, 65, 67, 68, 85–88, 89, 91—92, 93–95, 103–104; friends of, 104–105; health of, 92–93; occupational history of, 62–63, 97, 98–103; on reciprocity, 105–106; training of, 57, 96–97
Santiago, 89. *See also* Gran Santiago
Schedules: teaching, 60–61, 82–83, 98, 120
Scholarships, 103

Schools, 113; budgets of, 139–140; establishment of, 53–54, 94; municipalization of, 41–43, 61–62, 98–99, 120, 141; private, 22, 40, 50–51, 56, 58–59, 60, 76, 135–136; public, 1, 22, 50, 88
Secondary schools. See High schools
Secretariats: regional, 44
Self-concept: of teachers, 68–69
Services, 3, 9, 22, 25, 30
Service sector, 15, 17
Servicio de Viviendas, 132
SIMCE. See Sistema de Medición de la Calidad de la Educación
Simpatía, 24
Sindicato Único de Trabajadores de la Educación (SUTE), 36, 116
Sistema de Medición de la Calidad de la Educación (SIMCE), 44
Skills, 14, 100
Social class: definition of, 9–10, 15–16; determination of, 10–11; industrialization and, 12–13
Social distance, 24, 25, 28, 29
Socialization, 14
Social Life of a Modern Community, The (Warner and Hunt), 9
Social mobility, 55
Social security, 3, 148
Social stratification: theories of, 9–11
Sociedad Constructora de Establecimientos Educacionales, 56
Solidarity, 26, 83, 145
Sostenedores, 35, 76, 83
Spaces: creation of, 54
Standards: middle class, 22–23
Strikes: by treachers, 98–99
Students: needs of, 61–62
Study groups, 35, 70, 108, 114
Subsidies: private school, 40, 54, 58–59, 76, 139
SUTE. See Sindicato Único de Trabajadores de la Educación
Symbolism: class, 16
System for Measuring the Quality of Education. See Sistema de Medición de la Calidad de la Educación
Szelenyi, I., 12

Talca, 127
Talleres de Educación Democrátic (TED), 108
Teachers, 1, 19, 31, 36, 37, 46, 66; economic situation of, 112–113, 149; employment of, 34–35; in family, 55, 56, 85_87; interactions of, 119–120, 122; living conditions of, 45, 136; qualification of, 56–57; salaries of, 38 (table), 40, 135–136, 137, 138–139, 141; self-concept of, 68–609; on state's role, 43–44; training of, 33, 39–40; voluntary contributions of, 143–144; working conditions of, 147–148
Teachers' Association. See Colegio de Profesores
Teachers' Day, 81, 83
Teacher-Training College. See Escuela Normal
Teaching: level of, 113–114; as profession, 142–143; vision of, 69–72
Teaching Career. See Carrera Docente
TED. See Talleres de Educación Democrátic
Tironi, Eugenio, 15–16
Torture, 51, 52
Touraine, Alain, 9, 11–12
Trade, 4, 17, 18
Training, 38; quality of, 71, 113–114; of teachers, 33, 39–40, 56–57, 74, 87, 96–97, 141–142; workshop, 59, 102
Tuition, 55, 58, 103, 126–127

Unemployment, 5, 6 (table), 52–53, 99–100
Unidades tributarias mensuales (UTM), 40
Unidad Popular (UP), 50, 66, 95, 119
Unification: symbolic, 16
Unión Comunal de Centros de Madres, 43
Unión Comunal de Juntas de Vecinos, 42–43
Unionism, 35, 81–82
Union of Centers for Mothers. See Unión Comunal de Centros de Madres
Union of Neighborhood Associations. See Unión Comunal de Juntas de Vecinos
Universidad Católica, 53, 57, 110, 113–114, 137, 139
Universidad de Chile, 33, 40, 51, 57, 115, 139
Universidad de La Serena, 114
Universidad de Santiago, 126–127

Universidad Metropolitana de Ciencias de la Educación, 40, 110
Universidad Técnica, 73, 126–127
Universities, 14, 57, 58, 90–91, 103
UP. *See* Unidad Popular
Urbanization, 14
Urban sector, 2, 15
UTM. *See Unidades tributarias mensuales*

Vacations, 103, 122
Vásquez, Rosario, 49, 50, 61
Vidal, Marcia, 65, 73; family of, 107–108; on living standards, 110–111; on municipalization, 61–62; occupational history of, 59, 60, 64, 108–109; schooling of, 56, 57–58; on teaching, 70, 71–72
Vidich, Arthur J., 10: *The New American Society*, 11
Viña, 95

Warner, W. Lloyd: *The Social Life of a Modern Community*, 9, 10–11
Weber, Max, 9, 12
Welfare state, 1, 3
Work. *See* Employment
Workshops, 59, 63, 99, 102–103, 108, 124

About the Book and the Authors

Over the past ten years, most Latin American countries have experienced dramatic economic changes as a result of their enormous debt burden, with a diminished economic role for the state and a consequent drastic cut in state social expenditures. The authors of this provocatice book explore the clearly negative impact of these changes on the middle class in Chile, where the military government was able to take draconian measures in applying the neoliberal model, without fear of political opposition.

Lomnitz and Melnick take as their case the transformation of the economic and social position of Chilean educators between the early 1970s and the late 1980s. As Chile's education system was decentralized, teachers lost all job security and saw their wages and working conditions decline. The quality of public education suffered, as well.

The authors are especially concerned with transformations in the teachers' social networks, finding them comparable now to those typical in a Mexican shantytown, as opposed to more traditional middle-class networks. Their statistical data enable the reader to grasp the broad sweep of contemporary middle class Chilean reality, while the personal stories they retell—revealing the voices of people who feel that their position and their dignity have been undermined—give life to this reality as experienced by individual Chileans.

Larissa A. Lomnitz is professor of cultural anthropology at the National University of Mexico. *Ana Melnick* is a radio journalist in Chile.

DUE DATE